More Than A Miracle

THE MINISTRY OF AFTERCARE

By Frank Costantino
as told to
Jeff Park

ISBN 0-912275-04-9
© 1985 by PTL Enterprises, Inc.

PTL Television Network
Charlotte, North Carolina 28279

All rights reserved. No part of this publication may be reproduced, stored in a retrieval system, or transmitted in any form or by any means without prior permission of the copyright owner.

Printed in Canada

Foreword

Prison ministries within the Florida Department of Corrections has always been a valued program within the scope of our daily operations and has positively influenced countless numbers of inmates.

Frank Costantino and Christian Prison Ministries has played a successful role in this ever-expanding program, turning the lives of many offenders around and helping them become law-abiding and productive members of society. The program has provided both spiritual and physical assistance to those offenders who have cried out for help.

More Than a Miracle is more than a simple account of the growth of Christian Prison Ministries. Not only is it a testament to the devotion and dedication of Frank Costantino and his associates in prison ministries, but a narrative full of hope and inspiration.

Frank has earned the respect and confidence of inmates, staff and State officials because of his continued commitment to improving the Department of Corrections and his unrelenting effort to broaden his ministries. Frank makes himself available to the Department when called upon. He has been a valued member of the Governor's Advisory Committee on Corrections. His insight into the problems of "aftercare" has been one of his major contributions.

The stories of some of the young men touched by the Christian Prison Ministries program are told in a forthright and inspiring light and it is my hope that you too may be inspired by *More Than a Miracle*.

LOUIE L. WAINWRIGHT
Secretary
Florida Department of Corrections

July 15, 1985

Contents

I.	Three That Hurt	1
II.	Looking For Lasting Fruit	5
III.	Avoiding the Truth	11
IV.	The Bon Ami Rubs Off	17
V.	O.K., I'll Do It, Now What?	21
VI.	Getting Priorities Right	25
VII.	Finally We Get To Build	31
VIII.	The Best Laid Plans of Mice and Men	35
IX.	Work—Curse or Blessing?	41
X.	A Man, A Husband, A Father	47
XI.	Coming Out of Deception	51
XII.	Keys to Leadership	57
XIII.	My Warden, My Adversary, My Friend	65
XIV.	Where Do We Go From Here?	73
Appendix B	Plain Talk in Hard Places	79
Appendix A	Application for The Bridge	85
Appendix C	Aftercare Center Directory	103

I.
Three That Hurt

If ever there was a Christian fanatic, it was Bill L. in the Florida State Prison. When I met Bill, he was a pure zealot for Jesus.

Incarcerated for child-molesting, Bill had come to Christ through our outreach there and the influence of Chaplain Max Jones. There was no doubt that Bill had experienced the miracle of conversion. His face radiated the joy of being born again. He rapidly became a leader in the prison church and witnessed daily to other inmates of his new faith. Numerous correspondence Bible study certificates in his cell attested to his sincerity.

When the time neared for his release from prison, Bill approached Chaplain Jones about going to a Christian environment on the outside. Because of his crime, his own family wanted nothing to do with him. Max immediately thought of our ministry and approached me about taking Bill. Knowing Bill's crime, I was more than a little hesitant, but I trusted Max's opinion implicitly—after all, he was the one who led me to Christ in prison eight years before. So when Max assured me that Bill's new life in Christ was on solid ground, I welcomed Bill to Orlando.

To start, my wife, Bunny, and I took Bill right into our home. He became an extended member of our family with our six children. Within just a few days, we were able to get Bill a steady job painting for a Christian contractor who was on our ministry board.

Everything seemed great for Bill. He joined our renewal prayer group and frequently shared and testified of God's goodness. As he got established, he moved out of our home and got a room of his own. But he still came by regularly and maintained close fellowship ties with Danny, his employer.

Bill trusted Danny and would share with him any tempting evil thoughts he had, and they would pray together for God's strength. Nevertheless, within a year of his release, in a nearby store one day, Bill accosted a child in the toy department. Bill ran but was immediately apprehended by the police. Bill caught another heavy prison sentence and is still in prison today.

What happened? Wasn't the power of Christ strong enough to deliver Bill from the old ways? Had Bill really changed or was it a game? All were questions I couldn't explain.

Tim was also from Florida State Prison. (When he had entered the joint, he had been a confused, drug-crazed young man, but all that had begun to change.) Tim had received Christ and was starting to receive counsel and help from Chaplain Jones.

Knowing that without some kind of outside help, he'd be right back into the streets and crime, Tim asked the chaplain about getting help in re-entry. So Max called me and said, "Listen, Frank, this kid is at a crossroads. He could go either way. Maybe if you could help him through, he'll make it."

What could I say? Besides Tim had been a friend of my brother, Bobby. So we took Tim into our home and got him a job immediately. At the time, I was traveling extensively in ministry, so we all agreed it best for Tim to get his own place. Close by, there was an elderly lady who rented Tim a private room at a reasonable cost. But Tim still came by to see us regularly.

Knowing the importance of Christian fellowship, we were glad to see Tim get involved in a local church which had a strong singles group. We didn't realize this would be his downfall. With a deeply bruised self-image from prison, Tim hungered for self-acceptance. (He found it most easily in a "fringe" person in the group—a woman also hungering for acceptance.) Soon they were sleeping together, ignoring God's standards for their lives. Guilt-ridden and confused by what was happening but unable to trust anyone enough to share his problem, Tim drifted from us, and more importantly, from God.

Eventually, Tim married a wealthy divorcee. She put him in charge of her construction company. So suddenly, Tim had fast money he hadn't worked to earn. He couldn't handle it and began running around, drinking, and before long, was entangled again in crime. The bubble burst with Tim winding up back in prison with a heavy sentence.

Tim was totally disillusioned with God, us, and himself.

When invited back to chapel, he scoffed, "That stuff don't work for me." Here was a man with a miracle. It apparently wasn't enough.

Equally disillusioned and shattered was the church and the singles group that had believed in Tim. No more jailbirds for them. They said, "We won't be taken in next time."

Whose fault was it? I couldn't figure it out and didn't want to think a lot about it, for fear maybe it was mine. Besides, there were too many good things happening in the ministry with scores of men and women being saved in prison weekly.

David came to us about the same time. He, too, had been saved in prison, was recommended to us by his chaplain, and wanted to parole in a Christian environment.

We set David up in an apartment, got him a job, and introduced him to some good Christian fellowship. Not knowing enough about David's past, it was some time before I even suspected David's drinking problem.

Late one Saturday night, we received a knock on the door to our home. It was David and his parole officer. David had been booked for aggravated assault, drunk and disorderly. Graciously the parole officer agreed not to pull David's parole if I would take him into my personal custody.

I confronted David with his drinking problem and demanded that he get counseling. This seemed to work for awhile, but then David started drinking again. Despite my warnings (and his parole officer's), David wound up breaking into a liquor store for booze. Instead of leaving with the goods, he sat down in the store for a snort, drank 'til he passed out, and awoke the next morning in jail charged with breaking and entering and burglary.

Back in the penitentiary, David called me and asked if I would use my personal influence to get the court and parole officer to drop the charges and release him back to me. I had to tell David that the only evidence I'd seen of his life is that he wanted God and the others to get him out of his problems; that he really wasn't facing them and working them through. Therefore, I would not even try to intervene.

Besides the parole violation, David caught another lengthy sentence. At last report, David was telling his fellow inmates that he was back in prison because I was mad at him for not going to church.

My name was "mud" for awhile at the joint, and I was tempted to become just like that local church and say, "You guys won't get me next time."

Instead, I pushed Bill, Tim and David into the back of my mind, along with the question, "Isn't the miracle of salvation enough for men in prison?"

II.
Looking For Lasting Fruit

It was the end of the year and time for my annual report to my bishop, William H. Folwell. Sitting at my desk, looking over ministry reports and expense stubs from my extensive travels, I thought, "1977 has surely been a blessed year."

In counting up services in both prisons and churches, I had spoken and given my testimony over 200 times. While I didn't have detailed records, I could conservatively report to the bishop that, with the help of the Holy Spirit, I had personally led over 1,000 people to salvation in Jesus Christ that year all across the country. My travel expense stubs alone had amounted to over $14,000, and God had provided it all.

There were other very rewarding thoughts in reviewing the year passing. I remembered that night earlier in the year when Bunny and I were sitting at home doing prisoner correspondence together. I glanced up at her and said, "Bunny, do you realize what this day is? This is the exact day twelve years ago that I was arrested for the burglary at the Miracle Mile fur store in Miami. Who could have believed that I, a professional thief, would be here tonight writing letters of encouragement to prisoners?" I could hardly believe my own testimony and all that God had done in those intervening years.

First, there had been the trial and the frightful awareness that finally I might have gotten myself into something too deep to buy my way out of. As a very successful thief, I had been a taker and was always able to take enough to buy what I needed, whether it was things, women, "class", a way out of trouble or whatever. I prided myself on being a smart thief—too smart to get caught—but at the Miracle Mile heist, I was caught red-handed, and the jury sentenced me to 22½ years in the Florida State Prison.

For a year and a half, I managed to stay free on appeals, continuing to steal and rob. Of all things, a newspaper editorial had brought my appeals to an abrupt halt and brought me to Florida State Prison, Raiford.

Two years in the joint made me sick of being a taker and sick of all the hate and misery around me. The only goodness was a chaplain who boldly declared, "I know that I know that I know that Jesus Christ is my personal Saviour."

That bold radical statement stuck in the back of my mind for months 'til one morning I found myself in Chaplain Max Jones' office saying, "My name's Frank Costantino, and I've got some questions I want to ask you."

Max replied, "Sit down and ask away. But first, how about a cup of coffee?"

A little cup of coffee, a caring listening ear, the simple message of God's love come down in flesh through Jesus Christ to redeem all mankind from their sin. Soon that hard, tough-guy, protective shield that hadn't let anything or anybody get to me, was cracking, and light began to break through my hardened soul.

The chaplain was saying, "Frank, before you go, I'd like to pray for you," and suddenly he was saying the words right out of my heart. "Jesus, Frank's looking for the truth, for something real, and he needs to see who the truth is, that it's you, Lord, he's looking for. He doesn't want this life he's had. So, Father, reveal to Frank your Son. Show him that what he's really looking for is your forgiveness, your gift of grace and love, Jesus Christ."

In that precious moment, I felt the presence of a living God for the first time ever. It was so amazing and yet so natural. I found myself praying too. "God," I said, "I hurt. If You care for me and want me, knowing what I've been and what I am, then take my life. I don't want it like this."

That was October 21, 1969, a day that God gave me not a second chance, but a new life. Jesus, by His Spirit, took up residence in my life, and for two years, filled me up with God's word. Then came my release from prison, reconciliation with Bunny, her coming to Christ, and a couple of years surviving, working in construction to make a living. Then I had opportunities to go back to prison, this time to minister, an appearance on a nationwide Christian TV program, and a vision to bring video evangelism into prison. The fulfillment of that vision came with more than 150 of the largest penal institutions in the country now equipped with video cassette recorders and sharing thousands of Christian teaching and testimony tapes each week. Then came recognition of the ministry and my ordination as a minister in the Episcopal church, a book of my testimony about to be published with a promised prison circulation of over 200,000, requests from prisons and churches to come and speak, and on and on.

"Oh, the faithfulness and goodness of our God," I thought, sitting in my office reflecting on all God had done. Surely His Spirit had led every step and each one new and exciting. What would be ahead? Maybe five thousand or even ten thousand souls could be won to Jesus through our ministry next year!

Among all these glowing thoughts, a little voice in my soul whispered, "Where are all the men and women that you led to Christ this year?" Thinking back over all those travels and the hundreds or even thousands of souls won to Jesus, where were they now? Were they still serving Jesus today?

Personally, I could think of less than a dozen ex-offenders that were really living a Christian life. Where were all the others? Were they having the same experiences upon release as Bill and Tim and David?

I knew nationally the problem was there. According to FBI records, 74% of all the offenders released from prison are rearrested within four years. Over half return for crimes committed within three weeks of their release. Eighty percent of all crimes are committed by ex-offenders. But what about those who've come to Christ?

I began to look hard for lasting fruit of God's work in the lives of inmates. In the prisons, the fruit seemed to be there in abundance and strength. Prison churches were growing as never before. In some institutions, as many as half of the population were involved in chapel services. Correspondence Bible studies, Christian literature and Bibles were coming into the prisons by the truckload. Some institutions were having to limit the quantities received.

Why then wasn't the fruit lasting after release from prison? I certainly didn't buy the argument of the cynics that we were just spreading "jailhouse religion" (imitation faith to impress prison officials in order to get early release). The conversions we saw in prison were genuine miracles of God's grace. Couldn't the miracle of God's Spirit working in their lives carry them through problems after prison? What more was necessary?

On the other side of the cynics, I heard Christians say, "If a man or a woman could make it as a Christian in prison, they could surely make it anywhere." I guess they were referring to the persecution that often comes from the other inmates when one comes to Christ. While this is true, I couldn't buy their argument in total either.

Actually, there are many areas where a prisoner's faith goes totally untested until release. For instance, take the areas of substance abuse and financial responsibility. More than 90% of all men and women in incarceration are there for crimes related either to theft or substance abuse. They had failed at making a responsible living or failed at hanging in there when things got tough and chose to try to escape with drugs or booze.

Once committed to prison, how are these people helped? We can begin by saying categorically that our present penal system in America is just that—punishment not correction. Our prisons do not correct. Says Supreme Court Justice Warren Burger, "We have developed systems of correction which do not correct...our systems produce the terrible results of boredom and frustration of empty hours and pointless existence." Echoes recent U.S. President Richard Nixon, "The American system for correcting and rehabilitating criminals presents a convincing case for failure."

Our criminal justice and prison system largely acts on the mandate of the American people. The mandate that we've given our prisons by priority is: first, control of the prison population to keep them from society; second, safety within the prisons; and third, if possible, rehabilitation. As a result, little effort is made to help correct inmates' deficiencies in responsible living.

Actually, most often the opposite happens. Through the idleness and frustration of incarceration, inmates learn to be less responsible. According to a recent psychological report, where the average adult makes hundreds of mental decisions every day, the average inmate makes less than thirty. Rather than receiving help to be more resourceful and self-motivated, all the material needs are provided for and rarely is there opportunity or incentives for improvement.

As for alcohol and drugs, taking them out of the environment doesn't solve the problem. It doesn't show them the destruction caused by substance abuse or deal with the peer influence of alcohol and drugs. Certainly, alcohol and drugs are available to a degree in prison but nothing like what they will face on the streets.

When released from prison, suddenly the ex-offender must face struggle, opposition, and temptation head-on. At least half of all released prisoners today will leave prison with no job. The state may provide them with anywhere from nothing to $100 to pay for both food and housing not only until they find a job but work long enough for a paycheck. So after years of having his or her material needs (bare as they are) provided for by the state, he or she is immediately expected to become almost miraculously self-sufficient and capable. For who wants to give an ex-con a job, whether he's found Christ or not?

When I was in the joint at Raiford, Marty, an older con who had served more than twenty years on a life sentence, got his release papers. He had worked up a home plan in Jacksonville and saved up a few dollars, so money was no immediate problem.

Marty went up to Jacksonville and wandered around for a few days, like he was in a foreign country. On his third day out, he caught a cab over to the warden's house and asked to be returned to prison.

For Marty, it wasn't even the problems on the outside that drove him back to prison. It was the paranoia, the "what ifs", the anticipation of having to deal with difficulties. The prison paranoia is so incredible that it ruins most people for life.

Consider the atmosphere of the average prison. Everything is so negative that any delay or irregularity produces gigantic negative jibes. Dear John letters, new warrants, turn downs by the parole board—nearly all the news in prison is bad. As a result, prisoners are drenched in negativity and they carry this negativity and paranoia with them upon release.

I don't know if Marty was a Christian, but would it have made that much difference? Certainly the Christian inmate learns the right information from the Bible—that he should get a job, that he shouldn't get drunk or do drugs, that he should go to church, and shouldn't give up. By filling himself with God's word, he can combat negativity and frustration.

By itself, however, reading the Bible or going to chapel won't give him marketable job skills or convince an employer to hire him. It will hardly prepare him for "respectable behavior" in the average main street church or qualify him to receive the kind of supportive help and friendship he needs from the church, because likely it isn't there.

Willie was finishing up an eighteen-year stretch (not his first) in Attica prison. Six years before, Willie had accepted Christ and it had dramatically changed his life. He was now an inmate leader in chapel, had a beautiful testimony, led the choir, and was loved by all his fellow inmates. As it neared time for his release, Willie got terribly depressed and discouraged. No amount of prayer or encouragement seemed to help. The morning before his scheduled release, the guards found Wille dead in his cell of an apparent heart attack. Willie knew he wasn't going to make it out on the streets again and couldn't bear to face that fact.

The fact that most prisoners, upon release, with or without Christ, are ill-prepared to re-enter the world of responsibility and freedom, was obvious. What could be done about that seemed to be that "more than a miracle" part. I wasn't sure I even wanted to know about that.

III.
Avoiding the Truth

Donald was one of the most enthusiastic Christians that we ever brought into our home. He had come from a very active and positive prison church. There was no doubt in his mind that God was real. In fact, he was sure that God could and would do anything he asked for in prayer.

We thought this was great, for a while. It did seem strange that every display of humanness on our part was treated as spiritual weakness by Donald. This came to a head one evening when our third daughter, Michelle, got sick with a very high fever. After we both prayed for her, Bunny called the doctor and got a prescription to relieve the fever.

This act totally devastated Donald. Almost in a blind rage, he blurted out, "How can you call yourselves Christians and then call a doctor? Don't you know Christians don't have to be sick? If you really believed in God, you'd ask Him and He would instantly heal your daughter!"

We came to realize that Donald's total exposure to Christianity was sitting in the prison church, listening to different outside groups testify Sunday after Sunday. These groups would share about what wonderful miracles God had done for them. But few, if any, shared their struggles, their doubts, or experiences in the valleys.

Donald came to believe and think that being a Christian was one constant mountain top experience. To discover that there would be trials to endure and patience to be learned in receiving answers to prayer in God's timing, was just too much for Donald. He had expected God to be his personal magic miracle worker to deliver him out of every troublesome situation instead of strengthening Donald's inner man to go through hardships.

Despite our counsel, encouragement and prayers, Donald couldn't, or perhaps wouldn't, see things as they really were. Every time that I would try to sit down with Donald, he would attack me with scriptures out of context. Disillusioned with God, Donald left, was soon back to drinking, and before long, was back in prison. Even if

Donald had been willing to stay, I saw that it would have taken patience and endurance to work through Donald's misconceptions. Time I wasn't sure I was willing to give.

About this time, NBC produced the TV documentary, "Scared Straight". The local affiliate director of community affairs invited me to a special airing of the film with correctional, community, and educational officials. After the showing, we were polled for our opinion. I was nearly alone in my negative viewpoint but expressed that I thought it was fear motivated, told a person what not to do but not what to do, and gave no positive support system for change. Therefore, while it may effectively warn some young people off crime's path, for the hurting and struggling delinquent offender, it only dug a deeper pit of condemnation.

Coming home from the gathering, a little voice in my mind asked the question, "How is your ministry different?" Sure, we were preaching a message of love and not fear, but how were we teaching men and women to live right and what kind of positive support system were we providing for their faith?

I tried to rationalize it out of my mind. Weren't we doing more than just preaching the Gospel of repentance? We did have an effective Bible teaching and training program through our video cassette outreach, providing dozens of hours of Bible teaching weekly for thousands of inmates. But what about Donald? He could quote scripture until "the cows came home."

Scripture information alone wasn't enough. I thought of the practical things I'd learned in life. Did I learn to play football by reading a book? Of course not. We learn most things in life through seeing another's example and then through our own practice and experience. Even educators agree that 70% of all education takes place outside the classroom. The Bible tells us that we "become better Christians and learn right from wrong by *practicing* doing right" (Heb. 5:14).

Where was the example, the practice field, the positive support system? Well, how about the prison church? Weren't we strengthening the chaplains to be better pastors and leaders? Just the year before, we had begun to sponsor chaplain retreats to provide them the strength of

Christian fellowship and spiritual nourishment. These retreats have been tremendously successful in renewing chaplains' faith and helping them build up their inmate churches.

But wasn't Donald from a strong inmate church? Certainly, there were many things about God's nature and loving one another that Donald and the others could learn in prison. But to ask a chaplain to train inmates to become responsible citizens while they are in a fishbowl environment where they essentially have no responsibility is like trying to teach a person to speak Spanish but giving him no opportunity to speak. It can't be done.

Effective pastoral ministry will be shaped about a man's current need. A dedicated, godly chaplain can help train inmates to live right before God in prison. But the prison world is so different from our "free" society, an ex-offender needs a whole other course of training to live in society.

The Biblical word for our teacher, the Holy Spirit, can be literally translated, "one who comes along side of." This is the picture of a tutor. In Biblical times, only the rich could afford teachers or tutors for their children. The tutor, teaching by example, would take the children to the marketplace and places of craftmaking and show them how it is done. This is still the most effective form of teaching today.

With over two-thirds of all inmates from broken homes, and most without any father image at all, who will give them what they never had before—like the value of fulfillment of work, how to handle money properly, how to relate to the opposite sex, how to be a friend without getting drunk or stoned? Lack of this training is one of the major reasons for all incarceration, and no chaplain can provide effective tutoring in these areas for all under his charge.

What about the inmates themselves, using the II Timothy 2:2 principle of committing help to faithful men to teach others? The idea was to find a small group of truly born-again and maturing inmates that would form the leadership of the inmate church. These then would be trained and discipled so they could go out and evangelize and disciple the rest of the inmate population.

The idea was great and basically scriptural. When it

comes to winning men to Christ and sharing scripture, this principle has and is working well in prison. However, it could not bring about wholeness and preparedness to responsible community living for two reasons. First, the inmate leadership were not "faithful" themselves, they had not successfully re-intergrated into the community themselves. One can't lead where he hasn't been. Second, as with the chaplain, these principles could not be effectively taught in an environment where they couldn't also be practiced.

How about then the prison ministry volunteer? Couldn't he be the needed tutor and positive support system? Through the great exposure of prison ministry to the church people like Chuck Colson and Chaplain Ray and ministries like CBN, Full Gospel, PTL and others, we are seeing God raise up a huge force of Christian volunteers to go into the prisons and minister. Could not this force be trained to be the effective bridging mechanism for inmates upon release?

Currently, most all Christian prison ministry volunteers provide one of three functions—witness evangelism, Bible study teaching, or individual inmate discipleship. All three services are necessary. The first two are chaplain and/or supportive functions. The third is the least glamorous, attracts the fewest volunteers, and is the most needed. The individual friendship made between an inmate and a Christian volunteer has strong potential to the needed bridge to community responsibility. Remember, everyone needs to be part of something.

What are the problems? First, there are too few prison ministry volunteers willing or capable of this. Second, restrictions in many penal institutions prohibit the use of volunteers in this capacity. Third, individual volunteers usually will not have the personal resources or expertise to handle the problems they'll encounter with an ex-offender.

Perhaps the volunteer can get his pastor or church leader to take that responsibility. Is the church pastor with a flock of 50 or even 500 prepared to focus constant attention on one needy sheep? Likely, nothing in his seminary training has prepared the pastor to effectively deal with an ex-offender. Perhaps, at best, in one course he had a guest lecturer tell about prison ministry or was invited to preach at a jail or prison occasionally. Not hardly the needed preparation for effective prison aftercare.

For example, some 85% of all prisoners have significant substance abuse problems. Many are from an intercity, interracial subculture. This is foreign to most pastors. So, no matter how compassionate and sincere the pastor, there remains a gulf between the average pastor and ex-offender. This gulf is not easily spanned by either person.

I found that many pastors would outwardly welcome the ex-offender to his church. But inwardly, they were thinking, "I'm going to have to watch this guy closely to make sure he doesn't contaminate our 'good' young people. If he makes one mistake, we'll just have to get rid of him." This does not mean to say all pastors feel this way. Our intention here is to show that a concerned pastor is going to be concerned about more than the one lost sheep. He is going to be concerned about the possible negative influence on the young people, some of whom may belong to him. But most of all, we want you to see how an ex-offender can represent a threat to the local church. A threat that has its foundation in some fear that is legitimate and some that is not.

Can the prison ministry volunteer handle the needs of ex-offenders alone? Only if through experience, he is trained and knowledgeable to provide proper care and discipline. For most, this experience comes only through the pain of having "one's lunch eaten" several times.

Not long ago, a woman came to me to see if I could help her pick up the pieces of her broken life. A bright, level-headed and spiritually mature woman, she had been working as a correspondent in a large prison ministry. Her problem was that she was married to a man she didn't really respect and with whom she couldn't share her work.

Over a period of months and even years, she developed a close friendship in correspondence with an inmate. She began to share her own emotional needs in a way that she wasn't able to do with her husband. When the inmate was released, she allowed herself to become romantically involved in an illicit affair. Knowing it was wrong and feeling disgraced in her own eyes and faith, she had quit the ministry and was coming to me to see if there was any remaining hope for her in God or her marriage.

Do not be deceived about this issue. This is not one isolated case; this is very common. If one were to take a concensus of prison wardens, chaplains and leaders of prison ministries, I venture 95% of them could tell stories similar to the one I just mentioned.

A major reason for writing this manual is so that this type of thing doesn't have to happen again and again. Too many good volunteers and church leaders have been deceived, ripped off and become battle weary in the school of hard knocks before getting the needed skills to disciple offenders and ex-offenders. Not only have we hurt and embittered good volunteers but soured many good churches toward prison ministry. We can little afford casualties like these if we are to fulfill God's command to the prisoner.

At this point in my thinking and search for another answer, I was all "rationalized out." The options for the needed bridge mechanism for ex-offenders were narrowed down. I was beginning to get a vision. What these men and women really needed was to be able to go from prison to a Christian training aftercare center, where they could learn job skills, social skills, and Christian discipline and fellowship under trained, experienced Christian counselors.

Was God speaking to me? Was He telling me to do something about this? I guess some people may have a direct divine hot line by which they hear exactly what God tells them to do. For me, it rarely happens that way. Most of my divine revelation flows out of my own failing attempts at doing His will. I call it "Bon Ami" vision. You know, the window is all clouded up, and you begin to rub and rub and gradually everything becomes clear.

For certain, God has shown me what wasn't working. I know I didn't have the whole picture of what would work, but it was time to stop avoiding the truth and begin rubbing to get a clear focus. Was the primary focus of my ministry about to change? If so, it would take a miracle and more.

IV.
The Bon Ami Rubs Off

As Christian Prison Ministries grew, the Lord began to give me favor with the denomination of which I was a part. Recognized for our outreach to prisoners, the Episcopal diocese had ordained me as a minister and had become a strong supporter in every way.

One day while I was in my bishop's office giving him an update on the ministry, he said, "Frank, we've had some money given to the diocese that we'd like to put to some good use. What would you do with, say, $25,000 if the diocese were to provide this to CPM?"

He continued, "Don't tell me now. Go and pray about it. Then get back to me in a few days."

Pray about it? I knew exactly what I would do with 25 G's. There were eighty requests on my desk for video cassette, some from the largest prisons in America. With this money and some matching local funds, we could fill at least half of these requests.

However, that gnawing feeling was there and almost screaming inside me. I couldn't avoid it any longer. That little voice was saying, "This money is for a center for aftercare—a bridge."

Still wrestling with this, the next day I shared the situation with my treasurer, Ted Poitras. He was encouraging, saying, "Frank, it's got to be the video cassette recorders. This is a ministry that God has given us, and we really need to move forward in it now. No way do we want to get involved in this aftercare business. We don't know anything about it. All we'd end up with is problems on top of problems."

I was relieved to hear this and determined in myself to shrug off those inner feelings again. Tomorrow I would call the bishop and let him know our need for video cassette players.

The next morning, I had hardly gotten into my office when Ted burst in. He was frightfully white and almost eerie-looking. I said, "Ted, what's happened to you? You look like you just got run over by a truck!"

"Worse than that, Frank," Ted stammered. "It was the Lord. I don't think I slept a wink last night. God started dealing with me about your aftercare center vision. I couldn't get it out of my mind all night. Frank, this is what God wants that money used for."

I knew He was right. I knew it all along, I just didn't want to rise up to the challenge. This little voice that goes off in my head has been with me ever since I can remember. It's the voice that tells you something is wrong even when you can't put your finger on it. I was talking to Nicky Cruz about the feeling or voice one day while he was waiting to go on the 700 Club. He called it "street saavy". Not long after, I was having breakfast with Joey Donato in Georgia. We were talking about that feeling and Joey said, "Most street people and wise guys learn to trust that feeling." He called it "drift sense". A psychologist might say it is our subconscious trying to communicate with our conscious. Regardless of what that phenomenon was, I knew Ted was right, and the Holy Spirit was dealing with him. The question I had to face was, what was I going to do with the challenge God had laid upon me?

The first thing I had to do was openly say, "This is what God is saying. Remember the principle of confessing Jesus as Saviour immediately after salvation? Confess Him before men and He will confess us before God."

I told Ted, "This is a large challenge. One that could financially jeopardize everything we've worked for, but I believe this is God's plan, His vision, and we have to go for it."

When I began to confess the vision, things really began to take shape. During the next week, the Lord showed me, in a dream, an actual aftercare center building under construction and spoke to my heart that aftercare was not to be "my ministry" but would be "His" focus on prison ministry in the 80's.

When I went and shared all this with the bishop, he received it as from God and felt a confirmation witness to this leading. He said, "Frank, this is so important and radical that I want you to share it with our Venture In Missions board yourself. I'll make all the necessary arrangements for you to meet with them."

Realizing I was now committing myself and Christian Prison Ministries to this new direction was scary. Construction costs alone of an aftercare center would be at least a half of a million dollars and much more to operate. How would we get the staff we needed? If the vision wasn't actually from God and didn't have His miraculous support, it would really pull the entire ministry under.

Praying about this, the Lord impressed me, "Don't ask for $25,000. Ask for $100,000." This became my Gideon's fleece. I prayed, "God, if You really want me to do this work, You're going to have to touch these men's hearts so that we can get this project started right."

I felt pretty confident until it came time to make my presentation. The missions board committee was hearing several requests that day. The applicant before me was a representative of a national organization who was requesting only $10,000 to start a hospital for migrant workers. The 30-member board of clergy and lay leaders had put the man through the wringer with interrogation. "How was the spending of this money going to glorify God?" one asked. "We don't want to become involved in politics, only human needs," another said. These guys weren't pulling any punches.

With my size and tough upbringing, not too many things unnerved me, but I was wishing I was better prepared. With wobbly knees, I stood and began to share with my brothers how the Lord had brought us to this request and what I felt they could do to help. With that, I sat down.

After a moment, a priest stood and addressed the other board members, "If God has truly spoken to Frank, we must do our part. Either we give all the $100,000 or we don't give anything."

Immediately, another brother stood and said, "I move we give Frank and Christian Prison Ministries $100,000 to start this aftercare center."

There was no discussion either way. The motion was called and carried unanimously. Then all thirty men stood and clapped and praised God for this step of faith.

All around me the men were saying, "Frank, we love you..." "We'll be praying for you..." "With God's help, you can do it." I was dumbfounded, and humbled before God for my lack of faith. I wasn't sure what the next step was, but I knew no matter what, I had passed a point where there was no turning back.

V.
O.K., I'll Do It, Now What?

I went back to my own board of directors at Christian Prison Ministries and told them, "Fellows, I am committing this ministry to a work that is not good business by all worldly standards. We are going to build an aftercare center for ex-offenders to bridge the gap from prison to responsible community living."

"We're going to have to build a large facility, and I don't know where we'll get all the money to build. We're committing ourselves to a program we don't have as yet. And I don't know of any other effective models to pattern our center after. Without God, it will surely fail and could pull our whole ministry under. But I'm convinced that it is something we must do."

This shaky presentation brought a very sober and hesitant response from the board. Echoing my own previous doubts, they said, "Frank, are you sure about this?"

I asked them each to pray about it daily for the next month and then give their answer. After that month, the board unanimously, but hesitantly, concurred to build the aftercare center and helped me draw up plans for a half-million dollar facility. We all agreed that before we needed a building, we needed a staff and a program.

"Coincidentally", just at that time, the Lord sent us a man with a pastor's heart. We had never needed this type of person at CPM before. Now, just when we had committed ourselves to the task of aftercare, the Lord, through one of our board members, sent a man for this need. On top of this, the Lord showed us another man who was a Christian psychologist who'd also been in prison. Surely this soul-doctor, who knew the hurts of prison himself, would be a blessing. These two men formed the foundation of our aftercare staff.

Meanwhile, I began to talk to other established prison ministries about aftercare. One of these was my good friend, Johnny Moffitt, who had started A Voice In The Wilderness prison ministry about the same time I started CPM. When I told Johnny what had happened and what I thought God was saying about aftercare, he said, "Frank, this has to be God. It would fulfill the greatest need in all prison ministry. What I'd like you to do is to come up and share this with a conference of our chaplains and prison ministry workers."

When I shared at the conference, all heartily concurred that it was a timely vision and the greatest need in prison ministry, but no one else was doing this nor even knew of anyone with an effective prisoner aftercare program.

I began to ask God, "How come?" Prison Ministry isn't new. Christians in this country have been ministering in prisons for decades. Recently, it did seem prison ministers were sharing more out of joy than out of duty. But why no aftercare ministry emphasis until now? Why was this going to be the prison ministry of the 80's?

My inner voice had another question for me. "What has been the area of Satan's greatest attack in this generation?"

I said, "Lord, that's easy. It has been the breakdown of the family and our moral fiber in society."

The voice continued, "That's true and that's why there is a need today for aftercare as never before. So many in prison today have never been taught how to live. And when they are released, they don't have caring families to return to as much as before. But I will fulfill my promise in Psalm 68:6, 'to set the solitary in families and to bring out those which are bound in chains'."

When the enemy comes in like a flood like he has in our generation, God has promised to raise up a standard against him (Isaiah 59:19). I believe that standard today is seen in the renewal movement. The renewed awareness of the power of the Holy Spirit has brought involvement of the whole church in ministry where previously most all the burden of ministry rested on the pastor.

Therefore, we have not only multiplied numbers in prison ministry, but churches are more receptive to assisting with human and material resources. So, these two opposing factors, the family breakdown and God's standard in the renewal movement, have largely contributed to the present timing and focus on aftercare.

The focus and awareness of the need was clearly recognized by others, but I couldn't find an effective model of prison aftercare. So I gave my two new staff members the task of researching any effective specialized programs that bridged hurting, needy people back to responsible behavior. I was just a little surprised by their finding.

The first effective model was a Christian community in Belgium. This group took in criminally and mentally insane patients and reported a tremendous success rate in restoring these people to wholeness.

Why were they successful? Well, first they were family oriented, bringing the patients into the structure of extended family. Also, the whole community was committed to this ministry. They all shared in the tutoring, correcting and responsibility-building process.

The second successful model was Teen Challenge. Though they are working primarily with drug addicts, the needs and goals of their clients are almost identical to ours (more than 8 of 10 prisoners have chemical abuse problems). So we looked closely at what made Teen Challenge work. The government had already documented that the "Jesus Factor" enabled more than 85% of Teen Challenge graduates to stay clean. We hoped God would give us similar success.

One of the best things about Teen Challenge was its ability to meet the person where he was. The average church would look at a drug addict and say, "Boy, you need to clean up your act. Put on some decent clothes, cut your hair, and get a job." Teen Challenge could look through the peripheral and address the real needs of love, concern, shelter, security, and forgiveness.

This same focus would be needed in our aftercare center. This had been made vividly clear to me through a very confused young lady. Earlier in my ministry, I had been invited to share my testimony at nearby Mount Verde High School. At the end of the assembly, a young lady came forward to talk with me and gloriously gave her heart to Jesus. She confessed that she had been a daily user of marijuana and other drugs and wanted God to set her free of this.

At the end of the summer, I received a letter from this same girl. She was very depressed and discouraged with her faith. Sheila wrote, "I started off fine. I was praying and reading the Bible. God really helped me with the temptation. But now I've failed.

"I've smoked pot three times since the day I prayed with you. The first two times I thought that God perhaps forgave me, but now I feel like I'm just not going to make it. It's hopeless and I'm miserable. I really wanted to be a Christian and serve the Lord."

Sheila wasn't looking at the 87 clean days that God had helped her achieve. She was duped into looking at the three bad days where she had slipped and failed. Eighty-seven out of 90 is a good percentage in any league. All Sheila needed was some encouragement and understanding of the grace and mercy of our great God, which he has provided for us in Christ, to get her totally free from her past.

This is the same kind of grace, mercy and understanding that ex-offenders need from the church. But I'm afraid most churches don't have the ability to meet ex-offenders where they are, any more than ex-offenders can meet the church where it is.

I was told the story of the young Pentecostal associate minister who was given the task of weekly visitation at the local prison farm. For nearly a year, he went faithfully to preach to the men but never had a single convert.

Finally, one of his messages got through to the biggest, toughest, meanest convict in the joint. He broke down, repented of his sins and was gloriously saved. This excited the young minister so much, he ran back to the church to tell everyone of the miracle.

The senior pastor decided he just had to see this. So he made arrangements to drive his associate out to visit the new convert. Sure enough, for over an hour the prisoner unraveled his sordid past and God's forgiveness, all during which time he blew cigarette smoke in the pastor's face.

As soon as they were back in the car, the senior pastor lit into the young associate, "The first thing you better do is to get that guy to stop smoking!"

The young pastor looked puzzled at the senior pastor and said, "But, pastor, don't you think the first thing we'd better do is to help him stop killing people?"

That is meeting people where they are. Little did I know that God was going to have to do some of this in my own life before I would be prepared to do the same with others.

VI.
Getting Priorities Right

The plans for the program were rapidly taking shape, I thought. We decided to call the aftercare center, "The Bridge", because that is what we hoped it would be—a bridge between prison and responsible, Christian living in society.

Since men outnumber women in prison thirty to one, we decided to focus on men in our first center. Recognizing that many problems before were caused by incomplete information of the prisoner's past, we developed a comprehensive application that would give us a broad picture of the person's history and needs. This application is given in Appendix A of this book.

History shows us that God always interacts with man on the basis of covenant no matter how often he fails. Also, God in his loving nature, never interferes with our free will or moves in our life without our permission. Therefore, as God's servants, we wanted a covenant or contract by which we could come to an agreement with the ex-offenders at The Bridge as to what he could expect from us as leaders and expect to achieve himself. It would also need to be one which we would keep no matter what.

To do this, we asked each potential resident to list all of his strengths and weaknesses. We would also list what we saw as observable strengths and weaknesses in his life. Then in those areas where we agreed there was a need for correction and improvement, we received his permission to speak into his life. In areas of strength, we would look for opportunities to practice and strengthen those to serve and help others. This contract is also shown in Appendix A.

From what God had spoken, we knew that we must create and maintain a family atmosphere at The Bridge. How large we could build the facility and still maintain that atmosphere we weren't sure. Therefore, we decided to build the facility in two stages. The first stage would accomodate 15-17 men, and then, when it was well established, we could enlarge the facility to hold 28-30 men.

We also wrestled with how long we thought the program

should last. At first, I thought that perhaps we could turn our residency over every 60 to 90 days. But very soon, I realized that it was totally idealistic to think that we could break strongholds of error and deceit that had been implanted over decades in a couple of months. We settled on the idea of taking men for a period of six months to a year, and perhaps some would need even more time than that.

With that rough semblance of a working program, I was ready to begin construction. But God still had some preliminary work to do—in me.

In the middle of another trying delay, I cried out in prayer, "God, why are you allowing all these problems? Aren't I doing all I can and giving everything in me to this ministry?"

Uh-oh, that little inner voice was speaking again. "That's exactly the problem. And you better start working on getting it solved before you start building."

I knew exactly what the Lord was talking about.

When I had come to the Lord in prison, my marriage to Bunny was in a shambles. But soon afterwards, Bunny had come to Christ, too, and after my release, God began to put our marriage back together. Before this, I had never even tried to make our marriage work. And this was one of the first things God showed me I had to do. In many ways, I had deeply hurt Bunny. Some wounds are so deep that the mind will not focus on them. These are the wounds of the spirit.

What could heal these? Time alone does not heal them. I had to show Bunny that indeed I had changed, that I cared about her and would not hurt her again. With God's help through prayer, this really worked. Our marriage was well on its way to total recovery.

However, of late, I had begun to let the demands of the ministry totally rule my life. I'd be off running around the country, ministering in prisons and churches, about half of the month. Then when I was home, I'd work 12 to 15 hours a day without hardly seeing the family. When I'd dash off after supper, Bunny would say, "Where are you going to play God tonight?"

Not only was Bunny striving for attention, but she could

see that our six children, three of whom were teenagers at the time, desperately needed more of my attention. Understandably, Bunny and I began to drift apart. Our communication became nil, creating a vacuum for half truths, doubts, and fears.

I had all the right words, "Honey, I've got to do God's work. He's called me to this ministry and souls are at stake. We all have to sacrifice." So Bunny and the family sacrificed while I ministered.

With my own marriage on the verge of breaking up, I was glibly preparing these aftercare principles that I learned from one of Peter Lord's ministry seminars:

Point One: The men must first learn to take care of themselves and their own souls.

Point Two: The men must then learn to care for and be responsible for their families.

Point Three: Only then is a man prepared and free to serve others.

Hypocrite! How could I pretend to be God's man to minister to the world when I was totally ignoring my own wife and family? I had to turn around again and face my own failure. God was requiring me to walk these truths before I could talk them.

This is a hard lesson for any minister to learn.

Since I was in prison during five years of the children's formative years, it was easier to just let Bunny continue to take the responsibility with the kids after my release. Repenting of shirking my family responsibilities and "reintroducing" myself to my wife and children was terribly humbling.

It was worse at the office. I had to admit I was not the superstar who could go all hours and still keep the bases covered. It meant turning down many appealing ministry opportunities to take the additional time with my family.

Though hard at first, this has reaped dividends. The ministry no longer rules me. It's God's ministry, and He is in control. He will keep it going, with or without me. Now I rest at night in perfect peace with both the present and future in His hands.

God is continuing to heal our marriage. As I am learning to submit and obey the Lord to give more attention to Bunny, her own ministry has grown and flourished. Not long ago, Bunny wrote a book from her experiences as a social outcast, being the wife of an inmate. The book is called *Lady In The Shadow,* and it has given Bunny tremendous opportunities to minister to inmate wives and families. Bunny has been wonderfully used of God, and literally hundreds of inmate families have been helped, resulting in a greater strength and wholeness to both our marriage and ministry than I thought possible.

Nothing fosters Christian growth like involvement in ministry. This is why it is important for both partners in marriage to share in ministry. When only one partner is involved, there easily becomes a growth gap. What happens is that when one partner is moving toward wholeness, the attraction of opposites diminishes and creates a schism. How many husbands look at their wives' zealous involvement with Christianity just as they would another lover because the church has caught much of the wife's attention that previously was reserved for him. This same thing can happen in ministry couples where the husband is a pastor and the wife is not so involved. The key to success is to grow together, intertwined with the Lord, so no schism occurs.

So much for God's preparatory dealings with me. But I wasn't alone. The Lord was working on each of our staff to get their priorities in order, so we could be pure and strong vessels through which He could work to help others.

For one of our staff, God had to work in the area of financial responsibility. The men coming out of prison would face tremendous financial pressures in trying to make ends meet. How could our staff teach men financial accountability when we were not believing God for our own financial needs or were being irresponsible in this area?

Before God was through pruning the branches of this area, off came our bookkeeper who had cunningly beat the ministry checkbook for over $1,000. Along came the office manager, who, convinced that I would not fire her no

VII.
Finally We Get to Build

Even before the foundation was poured, God began to send men to The Bridge. One of the first was Carmen Chandler. He had come to Florida to die. On the run from the police, the Mafia, and most of all, himself, Carmen was strung out on a $100/day heroin habit. Knowing a fellow doper in Orlando, Carmen came to "die in the sun."

Either out of pity or to try to get him off his back, the friend introduced Carmen to a former rock and roll songwriter, Ray Petersen. Now a born-again Christian, Ray witnessed to Carmen, but the only words that sunk in were, "I'm going to pray for you."

Carmen began to believe that Ray's praying was a curse. Now every time he shot dope, it only gave him headaches. Finally, after shooting up $300 worth of heroin at once and still unable to get high, Carmen cried out to God, "If you won't let me get a rush, at least let me die."

In that moment, he could feel himself leaving his body. Suddenly, he was saying, "Hey, God, wait a second, please. I'm not ready yet. Please give me another chance."

From inside came the voice, "Then give Me a chance. You can con others, but you can't con Me. I'm God. You're just using dope as an excuse. Try trusting Me instead."

Remembering now more of Ray's witnessing to him, Carmen asked Jesus to forgive him and take away his sins. A beautiful peace came over him, and he was instantly delivered from drugs. With Ray's help, Carmen was able to get a room in a boarding house and a Bible. After a week of renewing himself spiritually as well as physically, he decided it was time to go out and hunt up a job, only he couldn't find one to his liking.

Ray suggested that he come over to CPM, that perhaps we could help. Ed, our pastor/job specialist, met with Carmen and then proceeded to line him up with a job as a laborer. After many years of high and fast living, Carmen wasn't ready to stoop to digging ditches. He said, "Ed, I don't need this. See you later."

"Wait a minute, Sonny," Ed ordered. Looking right into Carmen's sunken eyes, he said, "Before you leave, I just want you to know this is your last chance. Take it or leave it." Carmen took it and was on his way to total healing.

CPM and The Bridge (as it was built) became Carmen's daily support system. We prayed, hollered, laughed and cried through his ups and downs. Today Carmen is clean, working, and going to Bible school in the evenings. He says, "I couldn't have made it without The Bridge. Every time before, I'd get out of the joint with the best intentions. I was just fooling myself, though. These guys helped me face who I really was—a creep—and they still loved me through it all. The Bridge was my life raft when I was a drowning rat."

Not everyone saw The Bridge as a life raft. For instance, our neighbors. Now you can't expect too many folks to get excited about having a couple dozen ex-cons moving in next door. We anticipated that we could possibly have trouble with the community, so we addressed this problem upfront. We purchased the property with the contingency that our facility zoning permit would be approved.

When the neighbors protested our facility, a public hearing was ordered before the Orange County Zoning Commission. Not only did the Commission approve our zoning permit, they declared, "We hope that this will be just the first of many such programs to help those who need this type of care."

With this public support, we finally began the physical construction of The Bridge. One of the special moments for me during this time was to drive up to the construction site and see the exact picture of the vision of The Bridge that I'd seen in the Spirit many months before. What a dynamic reminder of God's faithfulness and guidance.

During the physical construction, the Lord showed us numerous important insights as to the physical surroundings for the men. Things like "homey" landscaping and warm earth-tone colors inside to keep from the institutional look.

Because men, especially Christians, tend to withdraw in prison, we purposely made most of the rooms as doubles. This would require the men to share and talk. We did build a few single rooms. These serve as rewards for exemplary and responsible behavior.

In the first phase, we had to choose between building either a kitchen or a recreational dining room. The Lord showed us the latter to be more important, so the men would have a place to eat together. We've since seen that how and with whom a man eats reveals much about him. We need only consider Judas' betrayal of Jesus to biblically substantiate this truth. Just as important is the strengthened bonds of friendship that develop over "breaking bread" together. Until the kitchen is completed in the second phase of construction, meals are catered and brought in to the men.

It was on a bright sunny day in March of 1981 that construction of the first phase of The Bridge was completed. Already several men had been sent to us, and were staying at the center and helping us to finish the construction. A few months later, we dedicated The Bridge aftercare center to God's glory.

At the dedication were friends and supporters of the ministry, a number of ministers, including my bishop, and several civic leaders. But perhaps the highlight of the dedication service was when Carmen stood and said, "I can't give you any religious message or theology. I just know that when I came here, I was a junkie. But now I'm free, straight, and serving my Jesus."

At that point, the Bishop turned to me and said, "How can you argue with that?"

You couldn't. It was a miracle, and there were many more to come. But we still had much to learn.

VIII.
The Best Laid Plans of Mice and Men

Driving up to The Bridge, one might think they are coming to a family home. The rather large parking lot, along with the two young men out front throwing a football while two others are chatting on the porch, suggest that perhaps this is a college fraternity house.

One enters The Bridge into a wide entry hall. Duty rosters and a bulletin board of area Christian activities line the hallway. It opens into a large living room that contains several couches neatly arranged to seat up to about thirty people for meetings, fellowship, etc.

Going down either hallway to the men's rooms, we see that the similarity to the typical college frat house ends. The rooms here are immaculately clean—the bed made and everything in the room in its proper place. Clean rooms are a basic start in learning responsibility. This is also a helpful incentive in qualifying for a monthly home furlough. No clean room, no furlough. So there is rarely a dirty room.

So far in our tour, things are pretty much as we had planned them to be. However, when we meet and talk to the men, we see changes...and more changes...and more.

When The Bridge opened, we planned to take only men released from prison on parole. We've wound up taking men mostly before their release from prison or state contract (more on this later), but also some released from jail, and some who were having difficulty making it on their own in society. We've even taken a few who were never in prison, but desperately needed The Bridge support structure. We call this preventive maintenance.

We planned to work with young men only. We thought they would be the most teachable with the most potential for change. Meeting the men now, we encounter men from 18 to 58 and everywhere in between. True, the majority of the men are in their twenties, but we have been open to teachable hearts at any age.

We planned to take only Christian men. We've come to the decision that we will accept anyone who sincerely wants to change his life for good, but doesn't know how to do it himself. Our primary concern in applicants then is a teachable spirit.

At first, we planned to use all professional staff. The experienced pastor and the psychologist that we hired both did excellent jobs in building the foundational program for The Bridge. However, after the men arrived and we gained some experience, the Lord directed us into a different staffing pattern.

We now have five men on staff, two of whom the world might call "unprofessional" people. We learned from Teen Challenge that a mix of professional and "street-wise" leadership is best. The responsibilities of leadership are shared as one serves as counselor administrator, another as the screening and substance abuse counselor, the third as the intake and job specialist counselor, fourth as counselor assistant, and fifth as community senior pastor. Each of these men have different experience and talents, but each has a pastor's heart and a desire to disciple men unto Christ.

We meet Mike, our screening and substance abuse counselor, in the parking lot, checking out the engine of a car one of the men just bought. Mike himself was saved out of prison, alcoholism, and drug abuse.

It wasn't that Mike was bad, mean and ugly. It simply was that Mike was a failure, and in failing, his life gravitated to those things. How did Mike's life change from a failure to a winner and staff counselor at The Bridge?

Mike tells us: "In prison, I came to accept Jesus Christ as my Saviour, but I wasn't ready to admit that I was a failure and needed to serve Him in *His* way. After I got out of the joint, because I had a lot of God's word up in my head, I thought I could go out and save and disciple the world. When I tried, I fell flat on my face. It was a disaster.

"Eventually I probably would have given up totally and gone back to the joint, but some friends told me about Frank and about getting some real training if I really wanted to work for God.

"Well, Frank worked it out for me to go to Dunklin Memorial Camp for a year of training. While there, observing as a trainee, God really got a hold of my life. It wasn't just the wisdom, power and love with which Mickey and the others ministered. It was their sensitivity to the guidance and direction of the Holy Spirit.

"I realized that if I wanted that too, I would have to learn to wait on God and allow Him to break the stubbornness and hardness of my heart and make me teachable to His ways. I would have never grown or even asked God to do these things in my life if I hadn't spent a year in that godly environment to see the value and usefulness.

"I believe that so much of what I've learned about discernment and loving confrontation can only be learned by hands-on experience and observing others being used of God this way. This is why proper training is so important in this ministry."

The place that Mike referred to is Dunklin Memorial Camp, an alcoholic rehabilitation center operated by Rev. Mickey Evans. For nearly twenty years now, Mickey has done for alcoholics what Teen Challenge has done for drug addicts. Mickey has had real success with many of the men who complete the Dunklin program. His tools of success? Mickey teaches the men how to work, how to live with a wife and love her, how to forgive, how to pray, and how to deny yourself when necessary. Most of Mickey's teaching is done by example, in the classroom of life on the edge of Florida's swamps.

We also meet Tom Barfield, our employment specialist, in the parking lot. He has pulled in with the house van. Letting out several of the residents, he chastises two of the men for being a couple of minutes late to the pick-up stop. After saying hello, Tom tells us, "Sometimes I have to be a prod or even a thorn in their flesh. However, the men know I'm pushing them on because I love them and believe in what they can become with God."

Tom knows because there was no one there to prod him on as a youth. As a result, he spent many wasted years drinking and in a confused state, finally winding up in prison. It was there that he realized God cared, even if no one else did, and God had a plan for his life. After prison, Tom went on to earn a Master of Divinity degree. Rather than going into a regular pastorate, Tom felt called to go back to prison to minister to the "fourth world" people.

Says Tom, "These are the people of the streets and

broken homes who've never had a chance because no one has shown them God's love or taught them how to live as His children. The Bridge gives these young men a second chance to learn, grow, and become successful men, husbands, and fathers."

From the back of the house comes Mark Barth, The Bridge director and administrator, with a large tray filled with food his wife has cooked for the men's supper. Mark looks squeaky clean and indeed he is, having never served a day in the slammer. He had very little prison ministry background before coming to us, but does have a Master's degree in sociology and ten years experience in youth pastoring.

Mark and his wife Cindy first came to us as music ministers, but Mark's gift from God is a pastor's heart. While Tom concentrates on employment and discipline and Mike with emotional and mental confrontation and restoration, Mark sees the spiritual potential of every man. His love for them flows easily and naturally.

About his ministry, Mark says, "Much of our labor at the Bridge is preparing the soil of men's hearts, breaking down the walls of fear, pride, hurt and guilt so that they can have a teachable spirit before the Lord.

"Most of the men come with an unrealistic view of whom they really are. Some come with puffed up pride and others are beaten down with discouragement. With loving interaction and admonishment, we can break down the vain imaginations, and build up the broken in spirit."

As administrator and director, Mark helps plan the activities at The Bridge. According to Mark, "Essentially, all the men work Monday through Friday day jobs and some may work on Saturdays. Four evenings a week we have worship/study gatherings, the other evenings are "free" or unplanned. At first, we tried to have something each night, but we now realize that those free nights are very important. They help the men learn responsibility by their own choices of how they use them, whether to go shopping, do laundry, read and study, or attend a church or social function.

"On Sunday mornings and evenings, the men attend church here at The Bridge. Then on Tuesday and Thursday evenings, the men break up into small groups, meeting according to their discipleship level. Those in orientation meet with the orientation counselor to learn basic skills in prayer, Bible study, quiet time, house and job responsibilities, discipline and goal setting. Those in Level I meet with the substance abuse counselor and concentrate on learning to look at themselves in the light of God's standards and apply God's love, forgiveness, and truth in areas of shortcoming. Levels II and III are smaller groups that prepare the men for going home, with more emphasis on finances and family relationships. Then Wednesday evenings, the entire house meets together for a time of worship and teaching as the Holy Spirit directs. Like other things, we planned to have a set curriculum, but the Lord impressed us to teach as He reveals the needs of the men."

One last area where we've had a change in plans is so controversial that I hesitate to share it. Our original plans called for building relationships with several local churches and allowing the men to choose where they wanted to attend church, as long as they did attend church.

We haven't totally abandoned that plan, but as hard as we try to encourage and strengthen the men's bonds with a local church, those at The Bridge seem to be so much stronger. Many that have graduated from The Bridge continue to return and look upon the ministry as their church. Because of the emphasis on pastoral care, it really is a church, and we cannot hide from that fact any longer.

In some cases where we encouraged men to go out into the community and become part of a local church too fast, it has failed. Bill T. is a prime example. Converted in prison, Bill wanted to come to The Bridge. Because of the nature of his crime, the Department of Corrections wouldn't let him become a resident here. But after his release, he became a regular part of the program with regular fellowship, counseling, etc. We got Bill into a church, but it wasn't the same. Before long, Bill called us from the county jail, facing the same charge as before. As long as Bill was in the community he trusted, he did fine. Away from it, he was lost.

As an extension of The Bridge program for men like Bill that need extended development, we are planning to build apartments around The Bridge which they will be able to rent after completing the program. The Lord has just now sent us a pastor to lead The Bridge church which shall encompass the residents, graduates, and even community residents who want to commit themselves to the ministry fellowship.

Another possible alternative to starting a church in association with aftercare center would be to recruit Christian families to serve as prayer support families to the residents. Once paired up, the Christian family would be assigned to take the man to their church and to one social outing weekly and pray daily for him. The resident would then have a committed friend and a pre-introduction to church. This is especially helpful where you can recruit ethnic families to work with similar ethnic residents.

In all, not too much at The Bridge has remained as we originally planned. Over the past several years, we've seen the Lord correct and fine tune the program to His purposes. This is not to say that plans aren't good. Plans help us focus on the goals ahead just as prayer helps us focus on the answers we need. Just as God doesn't always answer our prayers the way we expect, we must remain flexible and sensitive to His Spirit with our plans. Nothing will help us with this like experience and hands-on training—seeing God at work in our lives and in control of every situation as we yield to Him.

Now let's meet some of the men at The Bridge and see God at work in their lives. We might just discover "more than a miracle."

IX.
Work—Curse or Blessing?

Prison experts say that a lack of employment and employment skills (including motivation) is the number one reason for so many ex-prisoners going back to prison. Teaching these skills is then a prime goal of The Bridge.

This sometimes presents quite a challenge. For example, take Eddie. He is the one who has just purchased a car, a slightly souped up '71 Plymouth, with his work release earnings. For Eddie, this is quite an achievement.

A handsome young man in his early twenties, Eddie had come to The Bridge as a way out of prison. Or so he thought. Eddie recalls, "Another prisoner told me about The Bridge. It sounded like a better environment than the other work release centers, and perhaps it would become a short-cut to the streets. So I applied when The Bridge screening counselor came to our unit to interview the men.

"At that time I wasn't a Christian and viewed Christians as I did everything else—something to be used. That's the way it had been for me all of my life. When I was very young, I was given up by my parents. As I drifted from family to family and then was finally adopted, I never felt wanted or needed.

"Life from my point of view as a boy filled with hurt and rejection was a war of either 'use others' or 'get used yourself.'

"It seemed to me that school education was only for public service or big office hotshots. Neither appealed to me. Street education, about how to 'get over on others,' was much more important. So, I quit school and worked only temporary manual jobs when I couldn't find means to survive otherwise. Most days were a blur of drugs, alcohol, rebellion, and getting in trouble.

"Getting caught and being given a three-year prison hitch was just one of the hazards of the way of life that I planned for myself. In prison, nobody cared about me which only strengthened my selfish conviction about life. In coming to The Bridge, I was sure that I'd have no problems getting over on 'these Christians'. Then I'd be back on the streets dealing drugs and running my con.

"I didn't care about anybody at The Bridge. What I didn't expect was that the people there would care about me. The counselors and other guys really showed an interest in me. They weren't just 'shining on'. They cared and didn't seem to mind doing it.

"In love, they would let me know about my wrong attitudes and acted like they believed in me. For the first time, I began to want to care and try to get my life together. But I couldn't do it myself, and when others tried to help me, I'd rebel at being told what to do.

"I realized what I really needed was God. So one night after Bible study, I gave it all to Jesus—my hurt, resentment, guilt and rebellion. Jesus came in and saved me and gave me a caring heart for others that I had never had before.

"Learning to care about others has made a difference in everything, especially at work. Work used to be something you did only when you couldn't get by hustling. Now I want to work and do good because I feel better about myself helping others. And I see myself getting ahead, too.

"This car that I've bought is the first thing that I've ever worked and saved to buy. I'm also saving to get an apartment as well as to make some needed restitution from my past.

"Without coming to The Bridge, I'm sure I couldn't have gotten a decent job and probably wouldn't have kept any job because I didn't care about anybody or anything."

Eddie's "pre-Bridge" attitude toward life and work is not unusual. National statistics affirm that most inmates have less than a high school education. Three out of four have no marketable job skill, and two out of three have never held a job for more than one year.

The majority of inmates come from broken homes without a fatherly example to teach them the value of working to get ahead or the inner satisfaction of doing a job well. Therefore they lack both the training and the motivation for gainful employment.

Having spent their whole lives hustling instead of working, it is not easy for many ex-prisoners to change their habits. Mike was an active member of the prison church at Glades Correctional Institution. Upon release, he came to

WORK—CURSE OR BLESSING?

Orlando to be near CPM. Having had painting experience in the joint, we got him more than one job. But Mike was so used to hustling, he always quit the jobs. Mike is now in Union Correctional Institution doing a 25-year stretch.

Shad was a lot like Mike; hustling was his downfall. Hustling in prison kept him on the fringes of the inmate church. When it was time for his release, we offered Shad the help of The Bridge. He chose to "hang loose" and hustle. Now he's back in the joint for life on a murder conviction.

How important is dealing with an inmate's employment needs after release? Let's consider the case of Onesimus from the Bible. He was an ex-con, converted in jail by the great apostle Paul. When it came time for his release, Paul was convinced that Onesimus needed aftercare. One aspect of Paul's letter to Philemon (Onesimus' ex-owner) was to ask him to accept Onesimus and give him work, housing, and Christian fellowship. Paul knew that, with help, a con could change, saying, "in time past, (Onesimus) was to thee unprofitable, but now is profitable to thee and to me" (Philemon 11).

Helping ex-cons with employment is just as important today. According to penal expert Leonard Tropin, helping with employment problems should be a main goal of correction. Says Tropin, "It is more productive for Congress and State Legislatures to look at other approaches to crime control than merely enlarging the (prison) system... such as the causative factors of unemployment, racism, poor education, family instability, and alienation. Chief among all, I would place employment."

For most inmates, obtaining employment upon release is even more difficult than before prison. Without solid employable job skills and with a prison record, most employers won't even consider them. For men especially, self-worth is largely identified with their job. So any feelings of self-worth still retained after incarceration tend to become further diminished by the inability to get a job. This will result in either deep depression or be compensated by a fake show of self-worth with fancy clothes, souped up cars, women, drugs, etc. This usually requires resorting to crime to acquire these facades.

Difficulty in finding employment becomes especially frustrating when the offender during incarceration invests significant time and effort into prison vocational schools only to find most employers discount them because of no on-the-job experience. Also frustrating for the released inmate with good job skills is having to take a dead-end job because he can't get a job in his own field. In this demoting job, he likely won't perform well because he is not motivated.

When I was in the Kissimee Road Prison and became eligible for work release, there was only one job available to me. It was a laborer position at Graves Construction Company making $2 an hour. I'd work all week at that job and earn less money than I was used to paying for a pair of shoes.

My job was to run the "Georgia backhoe"—hillbilly talk for a shovel. We were putting in concrete slabs, and the work was hard labor in the hot sun. Because I was a young Christian, I was often tempted to quit and pack it in.

Here I was, a major criminal, who had handled and spent million of dollars, working, no, laboring for substandard wages. The reality of my situation hit me one day when the owner of the company came by. His name was E.G. Graves, a short little guy who wore a crew cut and never smiled. I said, "Good morning, boss."

He turned around and sneered, "What's good about it?"

I put my shovel down as he walked by and had to control every impulse running through me not to just spin him around and ask him who he thought he was talking to. Rage boiled up in me and started festering. Only knowing my future and my family was at stake enabled me to hold it in, put my mask back on, and take out my anger on the dirt in front of me.

This is usually the only kind of job "opportunities" open to ex-offenders. The menial part of the job is not the problem. In fact, the good work record of attendance, respect, etc., that can be gained in a dead-end job is just as valuable as good job skills. The greatest trial is when the employer is degrading and uncaring.

This is why job preparedness training is an essential part of The Bridge program. This will include how to prepare for and act during a job interview, the importance of being on time for work and giving eight hours work for eight hours pay, and showing proper respect for authority, even when it is not deserved or returned.

We never send men out to apply for work, but always take them. Almost every man needs and appreciates that bit of moral support. Applying for work is for most, a new and frightful experience. However, when they go through with it and succeed, it is extremely faith building, and a vital part of the total self-image development.

Where the good aftercare employment counselor will really earn his keep is in building relationships with community employers. The task is three-fold—finding the obvious and hidden jobs available, selling employers on hiring the men, and finally offering a good quality product in the men's labors.

While at first you may entice an employer to hire your ex-offender because of LEAA federal tax credit advantages ($2000./year) and your guarantees of supervision, the key is building good on-going relationships through providing steady, hard-working employees. Each man at The Bridge realizes that not only his job is on the line by the way he performs but also the opportunity for others to come after him in the same position.

If the job counselor isn't sure about a man, he shouldn't try to pass him off on an employer who needs a skilled, capable employee. Nearly every prison minister, myself included, has been guilty of this. Before The Bridge opened, many of the men we referred didn't last a week or more, and in the process, ruined our opportunity to place other capable men with these employers.

Now we let every man prove himself in a low level job. As a result of following these procedures at The Bridge, our job finding process is much easier. We've built such a good reputation with numerous employers that they will continue to take our men. They find our men are steadier and more conscientious than other employees.

This is the way it should be, because through previous mistakes and failings, ex-offenders can learn valuable lessons. Evangelist pastor Dr. C.M. Ward tells the story of doing something less than honest in his first job as a teenager. Unable to live with his guilt, he went and confessed his fault to his employer, fully expecting to be fired. The wise employer told C.M., "No, I'm not going to fire you because I believe you're a better man now than before you did wrong. You now know that it doesn't pay, so you won't be tempted to do it again."

For the offender who is only sorry he got caught, he has learned nothing. But the offender who is genuinely sorry and repentant of his crimes has learned a valuable lesson that makes him profitable to his employer and fellow men.

Eddie's voluntary steps to become responsible and make restitution speak as loudly as any preacher's sermons. God can turn our mistakes into miracles and more.

X.
A Man, A Husband, A Father

This particular evening many of the guys in The Bridge have attended a singles' fellowship at a nearby church. Claude chose to stay at the house and read. He says, "I'm not sure that I'm ready for that yet."

Claude has been married several times. When he caught his last wife in bed with another man, he went crazy. He came to The Bridge on his last leg of a fifteen-year aggravated assault charge.

Says Claude, "In the world on the outside, I had a real tough guy image. But inside I was scared and always running from something. In jail I tried to keep up that hard shell, but a Christian volunteer worker befriended me and broke through all that facade. He got me started reading the Bible and thinking about the Lord. Soon after that I received Christ as my Saviour.

"I asked to come to The Bridge from Polk Correctional Center because I wanted to know Christ more. Since coming here, I've really learned a lot about the Lord—to become 'Christ-wise' instead of 'street-wise'.

"Most of all, I'm learning to become a responsible man. I'm learning that with God's help I can make intelligent decisions and take care of myself. I'm looking forward to getting out on my own to see that I really can be a man and a Christian.

"That is really important to me, especially if God ever blesses me with another marriage. You know, I used to love women, but I never knew how to be their friend or really care or be a responsible husband like I should have been. At The Bridge, the Lord has built me up so perhaps in time I can have a Christian family of my own."

Claude is not alone in his failure at marriage. Three out of four inmates who have been married are now or have been divorced. Only 11 out of the 146 men who have come to The Bridge so far still had their marriage intact.

We've said before that we learn best by example, and since most inmates are from broken homes, few have any experimental knowledge of what a good marriage is. Most of their concepts come from the false, stilted view of TV and Hollywood.

Even in my own childhood, all the heroes were loners—guys like the Lone Ranger, the Cisco Kid, the cowboys, the cops, the hoods. All these guys were tough, coming in and making the big score, winning the battle, and then going on to the next adventure.

As with all of us, my heroes set many of my life's patterns. I was tough, independent and uncaring until Christ intervened and changed my life. These patterns are now seen in my children—four of them were born prior to my coming to Christ and two afterwards. If you were to ask any of the first four whether they preferred to be with their daddy or to be alone, each would say alone or it doesn't matter. Ask either of the younger two and they'd say they'd much prefer daddy to be with them.

Today's Holywood heroes are still the tough guy loners—only more rebellious, more carnal, and even less family oriented. Today we laugh at the outdated *Father Knows Best, Ozzie & Harriet,* and *Leave It To Beaver* type shows.

Even for a person that has a fair marriage before incarceration, prison adds a tremendous strain upon it. In his cell, a man goes through the whole gamut of emotional trauma with fear, doubt, guilt, frustration and fantasy over his wife or his girlfriend. Besides this, when a man is incarcerated, his family is also sentenced to all kinds of social and economic hardships and shame.

This was the situation with Able and his family. A Hispanic, Able got sent to prison for stealing to try to keep his family alive. He loved them and they loved him, but with Able in prison hundreds of miles away from his family in Miami, communication became nil. It was complicated by the fact that neither Able nor his wife, Denise, spoke English well, and on a meager welfare stipend, there were no funds available for Able's wife to come visit him.

As a result, when Able came to The Bridge, his marriage was on the rocks, and he wasn't sure if he'd ever see them again. We were able to contact Able's wife and, with contributions from local believers, were able to get her and the children moved into an apartment in Orlando close to The Bridge. Bridge counselors Mike and Brenda spent many hours with Denise, helping her with the English language, taking her shopping, getting furniture and clothes for her and the children, and helping her grow in faith through Bible study and prayer.

Although Able had received Christ months earlier, when he got his family back and got a job to support them, a whole new radiance and joy filled Able's life. Today Able is a good plumber's helper, driving a company truck, and within two years, he will have a secure trade.

Unfortunately, many ex-offenders' problems with the opposite sex cannot be solved as easily as Able's. Most come to The Bridge with a warped and damaged view of women and how to relate to them. Some have been hurt and rejected by mothers or wives. Others have so digressed in their interaction with women that they are more frightened of them than the junior higher at his first dance. Still others see women as little more than a sex object.

For this reason, teaching on manhood, marriage, and duties of a husband and father are an integral part of our planned curriculum at The Bridge. More than just Bible teaching, we involve the men with The Bridge staff's married couples as much as possible. For the men to eat with a family, learning to be polite, comfortable and friendly with a woman is a valuable experience.

At The Bridge, two of our counselors, Mike and Mark, are married, and their wives, Brenda and Cindy, spend time at The Bridge. They are loved as sisters in Christ by the men; and they show forth a godly example of what a good wife can be.

For The Bridge residents that are married, their wives are invited to be involved in the program, too. That means they can attend some of the weekly evening studies. On visiting days, they are invited to stay for dinner and the worship time afterwards. Brenda and Cindy take time to get to know the wives and make themselves available to counsel them when necessary.

Recently, a Bridge resident and his wife approached one of our counselors and said, "We want our marriage to be just like yours, because you really love and care about each other. So we both want to accept Christ and have you pray for us and help us so our marriage can be more like what you have."

As men who are single get established at The Bridge,

they can begin attending the local church singles' fellowship. We don't allow dating when the men first enter The Bridge, stressing to the men that their lives must first be on solid ground before they can think about taking care of a family. After the men grow in character development, discipline and Bible teaching, some dating is permitted.

For most, this is a needed test of patience. We do remind them of God's promise that in His timing, He will set them in families. Only the rebellious need dwell alone (Psalm 68:6). The Bridge, for many, is also a "bridge" to the family.

XI.
Coming Out of Deception

Whenever we see Mike, our substance abuse counselor, Jimmy, one of the residents, is not far away. It is obvious that Jimmy is trying to learn and soak up everything he can. It is hard to believe that just six months ago Jimmy didn't think he even needed to come to The Bridge.

We weren't sure we wanted him, either. He had been a heroin addict for fourteen years. On top of that, he had spent the last six years in a tough prison in New England.

Jimmy relates his own story, "I'm from a Christian home but grew up very rebellious. In prison, I finally gave in and accepted Christ. Still I didn't face myself and my problems.

"The chaplain at the prison where I did time, knew of The Bridge and told me about it. So I convinced the Department of Corrections to approve my going there as part of my parole plan.

"When I came here, I still wasn't being honest. I acted like I was coming here just to get information on how to start my own drug abuse center. In prison I had designed a drug abuse program, and it sounded great on paper, but really I had no solid experience to help others or even myself. The people here at The Bridge weren't fooled. Since I wasn't ready to acknowledge my own need, I had to leave.

"Back in New England, the parole board approved my staying out as long as I continued in some form of personal counseling. So I got a job, conned my counselor, and soon was back to shooting dope.

"Before long I couldn't earn enough to pay for the drugs I was using. Would I continue to hide from my own need for help and go back to crime or what? After wrestling with myself for two days, I walked off my job and called my dad. I said, 'Dad, I'm a mess and need help!'

"Dad called Frank and said, 'Jimmy really needs your help and is ready to receive it. Will you let him come to The Bridge now?' Frank told Dad that his calling didn't mean anything. If I was really serious, I needed to call Frank myself.

"When Dad relayed the message, all my pride was gone. I called Frank and practically begged to come to The Bridge. Frank said, 'OK, but you need to be here by Monday.'

"I didn't wait until then. Dad helped me get on the next bus. I arrived at The Bridge on Saturday, started working on Monday, and have been clean ever since.

"The Bridge program has helped turn my attitudes around 180 degrees. The first thing I had to do was to confess my total weakness and total need for God's grace and mercy. That lifted the burden off me. Rather than trying to 'front' and pretend I'm somebody I'm not, I realize that *I am* somebody to the Lord.

"It now seems the Lord may be giving me my original desire to be involved in helping others with drug problems. But this time I'm learning to do it right—to be a servant rather than filling my head with far-fetched fantasy ideas of grandeur. I'm starting to help with things like maintenance and transportation, as well as giving my testimony. If you told me six months ago that I'd be happy being a servant to others, I'd have said that you were crazy."

Jimmy's situation and needs are among the most common encountered at The Bridge. About 85% of all inmates nationwide have had serious alcohol or drug abuse problems. In June, 1978, an HEW report declared that as many as 83% of all offenders in jail or prison had some sort of alcohol involvement in the crime for which they were incarcerated. Nearly every man that God has sent to us has had a substance abuse problem. As with Jimmy, not everyone would admit that they had such a problem.

Jimmy, however, came to a crossroads in life. Would he humble himself and ask another for help or continue to try to fool himself in lies of drugs and alcohol? Jimmy chose to humble himself, and that choice set him free and delivered him from the power of drugs.

When does use of alcohol or drugs become a problem? Almost always! Who uses these substances to work or create or even to rejoice? Rather, they are used to allay fears, release tension, escape problems, hide guilt, etc. As such, they establish a deadly habit pattern of avoiding life and its problems, rather than confronting, overcoming and living life.

Carlos is a handsome young man that came to The Bridge like he had the world by the tail. Convicted of selling drugs two years ago, he pulled his prison term at a correctional center that emphasizes a humanistic positive thinking approach to all problems. Carlos became convinced he could solve every difficulty in life through his own willpower and motivation.

Says Carlos, "I came to The Bridge because it was close to home and I thought it would be an easy way to finish my time. It's been just the opposite, at least the first couple of months. The pressure here was greater than I'd ever experienced before. The counselors and the men here weren't just talking 'hype', they were really living right and they were challenging me to live out my talk.

"The clincher that brought me to Christ was going home to Tampa on furlough. For the first time, I saw all the darkness and ugliness I'd been living under, because now I had been living around the light at The Bridge. In the past, drugs and my own rebellion had hidden the darkness.

"I saw I needed Christ and the support of my brothers at The Bridge. My desire now is to grow in the Lord so, I too, can reflect God's love and light to other youth deceived by drugs."

As was the case with Carlos, substance abuse is more the symptom than the problem. The root problem is deception so one doesn't deal with life and its challenges and difficulties. Substance abuse is one of those broad roads that Jesus said would lead to destruction. Overcoming substance abuse in Christ is the narrow way that leads to life.

One might ask, "Since prison takes away their use of drugs and alcohol, why isn't the problem dealt with then?" For many men, substance abuse continues to some degree during incarceration. But more importantly, most prison officials have their hands full just maintaining security so that they can offer little or no programs and counseling about substance abuse. Therefore, the problem, at best, lies dormant during incarceration.

When Jim M. came to The Bridge, he freely admitted that he had been a drug addict for more than ten years before incarceration. Basically, he never wanted to grow up.

Says Jim, "When I woke up in jail, it hit me that I had to do something with my life or I was going to die on drugs, having wasted my whole life. I started reading books on philosophy and religions. But inside I knew that what I really needed to do was to swallow my pride and humble myself before God. When I finally did that, Jesus set me free of my lies, fears, and guilt.

"Here at The Bridge, I'm learning how little I really know about God and life and being a man. But they tell me that's OK, because I'm growing and learning every day. God's going to bring me through this with a blessing, because I'm facing life every day with a clear mind and heart."

Jim's testimony shows us that in order to overcome substance abuse, one must not only acknowledge and reject deception, one must accept and apply the truth. The difference between Jim M. and Donald (whom we met in Chapter Three) is that when faced with the truth, Jim received it and Donald rejected it.

Jim's imputation of faith became eternal impartation when he received it as for himself, applying it to his heart and will in obedience. Donald wanted Jesus' imputation of faith to fit into his old wineskin (nature). As old wineskins do, it burst.

At The Bridge, our substance abuse counselor teaches weekly Bible studies for the men in Phase I (after orientation). Each week's study deals with proper and improper attitudes. It covers facing fears, controlling tempers, copping out, surrendering pride, ridding guilt, healing past hurts, respecting authority, and more. These classes not only give Biblical instruction and counsel, but there is also a lot of loving confrontation and homework assignments that focus on personal application. The goal is life formation. As an incentive for men to apply themselves in these studies, they cannot graduate to Phase II (with privileges of furloughs, less house responsibilities, etc.) until they have proven to the substance abuse counselor they are facing and dealing with their emotional weakness.

It would be nice to leave you with the rosy picture that we never have any alcohol or drug abuse problems with the men at The Bridge. Despite our rules (and those of the Department of Corrections), some men will try to get away with this.

If one of our counselors even remotely thinks that a resident might be using alcohol or drugs, we demand that the resident give us a urine sample (our local detox center will test for alcohol and drugs for a slight fee). The residents know that if a test is given and alcohol or drugs found, they will be back in prison and/or out of the program.

Rarely, then, do we have to go to this point, for the men will come in and confess their misdeed. Then we will, at least one time, work with them through discipline (house restriction, etc.) forgiveness, and correction.

Without a doubt, it is easier at first to just avoid one's problems than to learn to deal with them. Many men have built a lifetime habit of this, and it isn't easy for them to change. Therefore, the substance abuse counselor must be both bold and humble, strong and tender, point blank honest and yet encouraging. He must be ready to applaud the slightest progress and attack the slightest slacking off.

What is good for the goose is good for the gander. We remind the men that we in leadership have had our "miserable meantime", but the reward of freedom is worth it all. They are a miracle, and there is hope and grace sufficient to carry them through to total victory! Experienced and qualified leadership does make a difference!

XII.
Keys to Leadership

While in the formative stages of preparing this manual, Dr. James Bergland, a retired professor from Union Theological Seminary, came down from New York to visit The Bridge. After a couple of days, we got together for lunch. Over salad, he said, "Frank, I can see why The Bridge is so successful."

"You can?" I replied, slightly amazed that an academic like Dr. Bergland would understand and appreciate what we are trying to do. "Well, Jim, why do you think it is working?"

"Well, first it's not just something you're doing," he said. "It is one of the ministries that God has called the church to do. The ex-offender's journey back to society is a tough road, and aftercare is the church's work of hospitality. The scripture is filled with this call to God's people, like we see in I Kings 17:9-24, Matthew 18:5 and 25:31-46, Luke 24:13-35, and Romans 12:13. For the Christian, such hospitality is a spiritual calling, a holy task, a disciple's obedience. This hospitality of the Christian fellowship is as old as the Gospel and as new as the next ex-offender we meet.

"I see close parallels between life at The Bridge and the early church community and am reminded of the ancient 13th century writings of a monk named Benedict. He described how they would receive traveling guests at the monastery:

'The guest is to be met promptly and with true joy. Since the risk of a mistake in hospitality is always present (Is this merely an adventurer, a parasite, a follower of some demon?) one then engages the guest in simple prayer. Thus not only is the guest introduced to the most important aspect of his stay, common prayer, but the adversary of the devil is chased away. Then there can be the embrace and the sharing of peace, followed by personal contact with others in the community. He is shown to his room, provided with water with which to be refreshed, and instructed about the ongoing quietness and work of the community. In this quietness the guest is

to listen for the word God has for him; his meditations are on the Book whose passages are pondered each day. He is invited to the common table, and asked to take part in the daily work. And when the time comes for the guest to leave, he is sent prayerfully and joyfully on his journey, as one walking onward in the presence of God.'

"Of course, here at The Bridge, the inmates' search is not just for food, shelter, and work, although it is the Lord's will that he has each of those. Ultimately, his quest is for God, a yearning for spiritual fellowship, a thirst for salvation. The Christian community has always been and is now called to this work of hospitality. Like with any calling, there are those uniquely gifted by the Holy Spirit and called to be trained so that the gifts of hospitality may truly be given to the glory of God. This is what is happening at The Bridge."

The best aftercare program in the world will fall on its face if it is not divinely called and led. And even a "weak" program can succeed if there is a godly leader obedient to the Spirit. Jesus' only program of discipleship was to choose twelve men to be with him (Mark 3:14).

What happens when leadership isn't called and properly trained? Satan, our enemy, can quickly get in and have a heyday. I've seen it happen more times than I would like to remember.

Not long after we opened The Bridge, Sister X made an appointment to meet me at our offices. When she arrived, she explained, "Frank, we have got our own prison ministry going now in (a city near Orlando). For the past six months, we have been going into the city jail to hold services, and now we've started a weekly service at the correctional center.

"We heard about The Bridge, and that's just what we want to do. We know we can get a building and start it right away. We thought maybe you'd show us around The Bridge today so we'd know how to operate ours when we start it."

"Sister," I said, "I'm really glad you're interested in helping in that way, but the first thing you'll need is a godly counselor/director for the men you receive."

Sister X quickly responded, "That's no problem. Brother James Y, who's an inmate at the correctional center, is getting out sometime next month, and he's going to be the director."

Forcing myself to remain calm, I asked, "Ma'am, what makes you think that James is qualified to be an aftercare counselor or director?"

"Why, of course he is," she bantered. "You ought to see him. He knows as much scripture as I do. He's even teaching a Bible study and witnessing at the center."

I never could explain to Sister X that Brother James' inability to live as an upright citizen himself would prevent him from leading others into that position, at least until he first proved himself fit for leadership according to I Timothy 3:1-7. At last report, Sister X was taking her ministry in another direction, so perhaps no damage was done. However, many halfway houses and aftercare centers have started with ill-prepared leadership, bringing disastrous results to both the leaders and the residents.

Who then is qualified to disciple and lead an aftercare center and how does one get qualified? I believe that first, one must be spiritually mature, and second, there is no substitute for "hands-on" training and experience. This is why we maintain "trainee" positions at The Bridge so there can be a continual spinoff of leadership.

Regarding spiritual maturity, there are certain Biblical principles, or perhaps actually, aptitudes that characterize those God has chosen for this task just as the Bible describes aptitudes for deacons.

The first aptitude is a strong prayer life: "the fervent prayer of a righteous man availeth much" (James 5:17). A strong assurance that God is hearing and answering prayer is absolutely vital. The best program in the world cannot compare to what one touch from God's Spirit can do to change life.

Peter Lord tells us the story of the deacon in his church that he took on as a project. He recognized that though the man was a faithful attender of church every Sunday and Wednesday for over 10 years, he still wasn't saved. Peter was sure that the man had heard over a thousand of his sermons.

Then one week Peter was called out of town. The man came by the church office for something. While there, one of the church laymen prayed for this man. God's Spirit came upon him and he got saved, healed, and totally turned around to God. One touch from God was worth more than a thousand sermons.

Prayerful intercession will produce a stronger wall of protection and blessing than locked doors of stringent rules. Prayer will bring divine revelation and insight to inner needs and problems of each resident.

Most of all, the example of consistent, believing prayer will draw the men to discover powerful living for themselves. To train residents to talk to God and listen to hear God's voice should be the goal of every aftercare counselor. This can't be taught out of a textbook but must be taught by example and practice.

A second aptitude is consistent love and discipline. God's love alone is capable of the needed discipline that produces the "peaceable fruit of righteousness."

To have the strength and courage necessary to confront error and invoke discipline, one must be assured that God has placed him in that position of authority. Actually, it is the position of a servant—as a shepherd gives himself for his sheep or a father serves to love, lead, and guide his children.

Moving into such a position involves a maturization process, and one might never feel really there or strong enough. That attitude, though, is better than when one is too cocksure of himself. Like the man who went to his pastor and said, "Pastor, God has called me to be a prophet." The pastor wisely replied to the young man, "Please share with me, son, all the little things you have been faithful in so that God would raise you up to such a high calling."

If we have not had our own maturization process in the trenches, we cannot lead others out.

One must recognize, too, that discipline and correction are good. God says "He scourges all that He loves" (Heb. 12:6). It is no fun to be corrected or even to be the corrector. If, however, correction is administered properly, the residents will see that it's done because you care and want the best for them. You may be the first person who ever cared enough to correct them. They may not understand at first, but when they do, you'll have a friend for life.

Discipline must be both regular and consistent among the residents. If it isn't, the residents will learn to connive to get around it or get the preferential treatment or will come to rebel against all discipline. It is very tempting to let certain problems or shortcomings slide by. Don't! Keep short accounts with every man.

Pray about every problem and then bring loving confrontation. Never let a problem grow where it can cause an explosion that ruins the relationship and weakens one's leadership with the others.

A third aptitude is a balanced life; one who can both hear from God and also rest and recreate. So many men come to The Bridge with a "pious, super-spiritual" misconception of what Christian life is all about. They need to be shown that one can walk with Christ and enjoy the world that God has created.

A good counselor will be able to play many roles in relation to the men he serves. At first, he may be as a spiritual father to the new born or young Christian; then he may be as the older brother; and finally as a close friend. In each of these roles, he will have opportunity to build trust through things like playing touch football, pumping some iron, sharing advice on a car deal, or maybe sharing the excitement when a man finally makes that first car purchase. If one will participate in the natural non-judgemental activities of living together, the men will come to share their inner needs and feelings that couldn't be pulled out of the them with the threat of death.

A fourth aptitude is the ability to apply God's principles to everyday life, to preach Christ instead of conformity. Aftercare centers can easily become just another institution with a slightly different atmosphere and environment, or worse yet, just a flophouse. The goal is not conformity or even adaptability to the program so much as it is learning responsibility. It is very tempting to become directive, to tell the residents everything. When that happens, there is little real learning or maturity.

The old Chinese proverb says, "Give a man a fish and you feed him for a day. Teach him to fish and you feed him for a lifetime." We must be careful we are not just giving a way out of a man's current problem, but instead, are taking time to teach him how to deal with and go through the everyday trials of life.

Basic requirements for every man at The Bridge includes getting a driver's license and setting up a bank account—not just opening up a checking account, but keeping track of expenses, paying bills, budgeting, etc.

These are small but important steps toward responsible living. Residents that are maturing will be making more and more of their own decisions about how they're spending their money, free time, etc. Rather than being squeezed into the counselor's mold, they will be encouraged to develop their own gifts and talents. Growth requires change and change often brings pain. Men must learn to deal with and work through change and pain to its eventual reward. This again is taught best by example. How do we respond to problems, pressures, and changes? Do we look at them as opportunities for growth or do we resist and rebel? The men will follow our lead.

A fifth aptitude is simply experience—not being a novice in the things of the Lord and life. The job of the counselor/leader is not to reveal the truth. That is the job of the Holy Spirit. The leader, however, can and must confirm truth. The experience of faithfully receiving, appreciating, and utilizing the things of God gives strong credence to say, "Follow me."

One of the rules for all group sharing and discussion at The Bridge is that men cannot share what they haven't experienced personally. This cuts down on many frivolous, theological debates and doctrinal strife.

A sixth aptitude is contentment—the calm in the midst of the storm, the ability to handle the pressures of life. For many men, prison has been traumatic. They want no more pressures and will try at all costs to avoid it. However, unless they learn to face pressures, they will constantly be driven from pillar to post.

The leader must then exude peace—the kind of peace that comes when one is taking charge of one's environment instead of reacting to it. To enter a dark room and feel fear, then fully resist that fear and then turn on the light—that is taking control of the environment. Spiritual strength, peace and joy are all part of the inner man and can never be attained by outward human effort or reaction. Because none of us can avoid spiritual battles and pressures in life, we must learn to wage spiritual warfare, and having done all, stand in the Lord.

A seventh and last aptitude discussed here is a teachable spirit, one that is open and accessible to others. When we are properly related in the body of Christ, we realize that we aren't God's total answer to the planet earth, we are just one part of the total body of Christ.

When we want something from the kitchen, we don't send our hand in to get it for us. We take the whole body. Similarly, God, I believe, is not just speaking to me but His whole body about redemption of prisoners. Therefore, it profits me to relate to one another in the body so we can function properly and effectively according to the gifts of His Spirit in us.

Perhaps the most rewarding thing happening in my life right now is seeing God bring together leading prison ministries from around the country in C.O.P.E. (Coalition of Prison Evangelists). After five years of fervent prayer this has finally happened. We are learning to relate, communicate, and support one another, so together we can fulfill God's calling in this area.

One last thought on being teachable. When we are setting God's desires above our own, we will leave the results to God. We must remember that even God's perfect plan of discipleship with Jesus and the twelve didn't have 100% success as we might view success.

I've come to the conclusion that our yardstick for success can only be measured by our willingness to obey God. This was brought home to me while ministering at a Charismatic church a few years ago. In the middle of my message, out popped the statement from my mouth, "Anyone who comes to the altar right now, the Lord says He will heal them."

Immediately, I panicked and wanted to take those words back. Sure enough, up popped an elderly lady from the back of the church with a white cane with a red tip. "Tap, tap, tap" came that blind lady to the altar, and with each step, I was getting more nervous. What if she doesn't get healed? What if. . .?

Inside, God's voice said, "Did you invite her down?" "No, Lord," I argued, "I wouldn't do anything that stupid." "Well, then," the voice continued, "just pray for her and get out of the way." I did and was the most surprised person in the place when suddenly she dropped her cane and said, "I can see, I can see!"

All the way home, I tried to figure out why that happened. It sure wasn't my spirituality (just before my message I had fought with Bunny). But in any case, it wasn't long before I saw myself as the great healer, who even healed the blind, only I soon found out that God's healing didn't always work through me. Some people would be healed when I'd pray for them and others wouldn't be. And no spiritual formula would tell me why some would and others would not.

One night when I was really discouraged that despite fervent prayer this particular person wasn't healed, the Holy Spirit encouraged me. He said, "Frank, leave it to me. Anyone who accepts the blame when someone isn't healed will also accept the credit when one is healed. It is Mine."

I believe that applies, not just to healing, but to all our efforts for God's kingdom. When it comes to results, I like what Mickey Evans says, "I tell myself first that I'm not what I ought to be. Then I confess to man and to God that with His help, I'm not what I'll be tomorrow. And finally, I praise God I'm not what I used to be."

Obviously, there are other important aptitudes and attitude traits for effective aftercare leadership. It has only been possible to highlight certain key ones here. For those already in aftercare leadership or contemplating leadership, Appendix B, "Plain Talk in Hard Places", is added for you.

There is one additional subject that is more than an aptitude. It is a "dealing". It required a radical miracle to produce in my life, and I feel is so important that we've dedicated the next chapter to it—authority.

XIII.
My Warden, My Adversary, My Friend

Unless you've been an ex-con who has really tried to make good, I don't think you can appreciate the value or the difficulty in obtaining a total pardon. In my situation, I don't think it would have been possible without the help of some good friends. The Florida State Secretary of Corrections is Louie L. Wainwright. The following is the letter Louie wrote to the Clemency Board for me:

Mrs. Alice Ragsdale, Coordinator
Executive Clemency Board
Larson Building
Tallahassee, Florida 32301

RE: Frank Costantino

Dear Mrs. Ragsdale:
It is my understanding that Reverend Frank Costantino has made application to the Governor and Executive Clemency Board for pardon.
I knew Frank while he was serving his obligation for the crimes he committed against the State of Florida. During the time he was actually incarcerated, from March 5, 1968, until he was paroled on January 11, 1972, Frank made a conversion in his life.
His desire to transform himself from the person he was prior to being sentenced to prison led Frank to study for the ministry, and he has become an ordained minister. Through the use of his ministry, Frank's calling appears to be devoted to inmates incarcerated in jails and prisons with a high concentration of his being here in Florida.
Frank has worked very closely with our chaplains in trying to strengthen the religious programs within our department, as he has been able to complement and supplement some of the religious needs that we are unable to provide. Frank is constantly in and out of the various institutions with the Department of Corrections, servicing the religious needs through counseling, study services, and prayers. He has earned the respect of both

inmates and staff by the manner in which he conducts himself in his role as President of the Christian Prison Ministries, Inc.

Because of the change that was made by Frank in his life and in his dedication to assisting others, I appointed him to serve on the Executive Review Committee for the department. I later recommended and he was appointed by Governor Graham in March, 1981, to serve as a member of the Governor's Advisory Committee on Corrections. I believe that he has been of service to both committees and his advice and counsel has been sought and greatly valued.

In summary, Reverend Costantino was released from incarceration over ten years ago, and through the commitments that he made to change his life, he has been an asset to the Department of Corrections and the State of Florida. I support Frank in his applying for a pardon and submit this letter as my recommendation for the pardon. I will be happy to appear before the Clemency Board in his behalf if requested to do so.

Sincerely,
Louie L. Wainwright
Secretary

Louie and I go back a long time—but not always as friends. I entered into Louie's world on March 5, 1968. That was the day I entered Union Correctional Institution in Raiford to begin serving a 22½-year sentence for burglary. That day, Louie Wainwright, Secretary of Corrections, became my keeper.

In prison, I wasn't the model inmate by any means. An accomplished thief, I was used to getting my own way. So before meeting the Lord in the joint, I was constantly running a con to get my way and to get over on others. That doesn't make one very popular with the prison administrators.

When God's love finally reached me through Chaplain Max Jones, I repented and received Jesus Christ as my Saviour and Lord. My feelings, however, didn't automatically change toward my keepers.

As a young Christian in prison, I continued to look at the prison system as my adversary, without knowledge that the help I was receiving through the chaplain was being made possible by the system that I was resisting. In ignorance, I viewed the prison administration as the bad guys, keeping men caged up as animals—opposite to Jesus' ministry of setting the captive free.

This view was reinforced by most of the Christian groups who came to prison to minister to us. These people were usually cooperative with our chaplain but often acted as if the guards and administrators had the plague or weren't worth giving the time of day.

Unfortunately, this is still true of many prison ministries today. They desire to give the ministry of love but don't have the proper respect for the ministry of the law, without which our prisons would be total chaos with no opportunity to minister love. The Bible acknowledges that the ministry of the law and its penalties are needed for the rebellious: "We know that the law is good if a man uses it lawfully; knowing this, that the law is not made for righteous men, but the lawless and disobedient, for the ungodly and for sinners" (I Tim. 1:8,9). God is on the side of law and authority: "Let every soul be subject unto the higher powers. For there is no power but of God: the powers that are ordained by God. Whosoever therefore resisteth the power, resisteth the obedience of God...for He is a minister of God to thee for good" (Rom. 13:1,2,4).

I didn't have proper respect for the huge task of the Department of Corrections, and I carried my errant inmate view of authority right out of the prison. When God began to deal with me to return to prison to minister, it was Secretary Wainwright's responsibility to approve my request. Why shouldn't he be more than a little skeptical of me? How was he to know if I was really sincere and not just running another con game with the DOC? Surely they had been burned by other ex-cons doing this. Nevertheless, I looked at Secretary Wainwright as my adversary in questioning my ministry to prisoners.

What I didn't realize was that all during this time, Louie was trying to help me. After investigating and checking me out, he used his influence to have me appointed to a six month task force, called the Governor's Advisory Council to Corrections (at the time, I didn't realize Louie was behind my appointment).

Then, when Governor Askew took office, I was appointed to the State Region Advisory Council to the Department of Corrections. On that council were sheriffs, judges, attorneys, and other prominent citizens—all of whom I had looked upon as adversaries in the past. Having to work with these people greatly affected my perspective of those in authority.

After the first year, I was elected chairman of the council. This required me to work closely with the governor's aide and top Department of Corrections officials. From this birds-eye view, I began to see the Herculean task of the DOC with its leaders groping for answers to an almost impossible situation.

I saw Louie for the first time in his own environment. Our council addressed from his viewpoint the problem of prison overcrowding, antiquated facilities, inadequate, underpaid staff, and a desperately stingy budget. Even without seeing all of Louie's day-to-day challenges of trying to keep 28 huge penal institutions functioning without exploding, I saw things in a new light.

Now I could see why it was sometimes hard to get the warden excited about some new chapel program when he was desperately trying to keep guard towers and stations covered. During one point in a decade when the Florida penal system was tripling in size, the DOC was experiencing a 55% yearly turnover in staff.

Being a decision maker myself, watching Louie in action grappling with these huge concerns, built in me respect for his courage and sincere interest in corrections. My attitude change became apparent to me when, about this time, I was approached by legislators investigating nepotism in the DOC. Instead of criticizing, I found myself refusing to get involved and resisting their witch hunt attitude.

When the new Governor (Graham) took office, a new Governor's Executive Review Committee on Corrections was appointed. It was chaired by Attorney General Jim Smith and included men like Dr. Merle Alexander (former head of federal prisons), Dr. Alan Alt (head of several DOC systems), and Tobie Simon, celebrated attorney who won the landmark Costello vs. Wainwright case. At the end of our six-month review and investigation, Attorney General Smith, Tobie Simon and myself were given the task of presenting our findings personally to the governor. As a committee, we unanimously voiced support of Secretary Wainwright, declaring that our state was indeed privileged to have a man of his caliber in this position.

This was a turning point for me. No longer did I see Secretary Wainwright as an adversary, but now as a respected corrections leader.

During the ensuing years on the Advisory Council, my friendship with Louie grew. I was able to discuss with him and his deputy director Dave Bachman my vision of an aftercare community working with prisoners in their last year of incarceration. Dave and Louie were extremely helpful, explaining the contractual and legal process, what the standards were, etc. They explained that two other organizations had such contracts of "pre-release service" with the state, and so we were able to follow closely their contract terms.

When it came time that the Lord encouraged me to appeal to the governor for a full pardon, not only did Louie write the aforementioned letter, dozens of other judges, attorneys, and government officials interceded in my behalf. In an almost unprecedented act, the governor declared for me a full pardon with specific privilege to carry firearms. For me, it wasn't so much that the privilege was important as was the statement it made—that God had totally restored my life in society—just as He promised. And the good guys that had been used to bring this about were the very establishment that I had resisted just years before.

In so doing, God broke down and removed the prison of rebellion from me. It was a rebellion that, at first, I even denied existed. But it was there (in that I resisted the delegated authority of God) and had to be removed before I (or anyone in Christian prison ministry) could work effectively with the DOC in pre-release aftercare contracts.

Under the contract we submitted to the state, once an

inmate reaches work release (minimum security) status, he can apply to come to The Bridge instead of a prison work release center. While at The Bridge, the Florida Department of Corrections pays a daily stipend for his care until his sentence is completed or he makes parole.

Since our contract with the state of Florida has been approved, most all the men at The Bridge have come under contract. This means that we must provide watchful security (really companionship), adhere to state rules, and submit monthly reports. But it also means that The Bridge has become nearly self-supporting. Instead of setting up a program in competition with the state and asking the Christian community to fund both by taxes and contributions, The Bridge's operating funds now come substantially from DOC tax dollars, all the while saving the state considerable expense because we charge 30% less than what it costs the state to care for its own men.

What about separation of church and state? There is no conflict. The Bridge provides a service of security, employment, transportation, work release and room and board for the state. The fact that we provide this with counseling in a Christian environment can only be viewed as an added plus.

Does The Bridge discriminate on the basis of faith? No. As mentioned before, almost half the men coming to The Bridge have not previously professed faith in Jesus Christ. While The Bridge has the right to reject any man who applies to come there, we look more at an honest heart that is open to change and correction than to what might be one's "religious jargon". We want men who want to do something with their lives and just don't know how.

How does a man come to The Bridge under state contract? When a man is eligible for work release status, he requests to come to his classification officer. He may have heard of The Bridge from his chaplain, a fellow inmate, a Christian prison ministry volunteer, or it may even be recommended by the classification officer. The classification officer then regularly submits a list of those wanting to come to The Bridge to our staff. Our screening counselor will then come and/or write to the institution and interview applicants before they are accepted.

Certainly, one of the most important ingredients of The Bridge's success is a screening counselor that is sensitive to the Holy Spirit. He says, "I can usually tell whether a man will benefit from The Bridge by the way he reacts to his problems and needs. Sometime during the interview, the Lord will show me what the man's needs and problems are. When I confront him with this, he will either acknowledge or deny and cover them up. This shows me his openness to change and the help we, through Christ, can offer.

"On an inmate interview, I will overextend the rules, making them sound harder than they are. (I also make it clear we are Christ-centered.) Interestingly, the hardness of the rules offends many 'Christian' inmates as nonbelievers. Many newly professing Christians don't think they need what The Bridge offers—until after they've been released and gotten into trouble. Then it may be too late.

"God has shown me that I must be patient. Some men will be open, and some will learn only after more mistakes. My job is to love and pray for each one no matter what his response."

Along with sensitivity to the Holy Spirit, every aftercare screening counselor must have a cooperative and respectful attitude toward prison officials. Our counselor continues, "I'm really grateful to Frank for taking me along to so many meetings with correction officials so I can gain the respect and understanding of the system's workings. Actually, it isn't all that complicated, working with the state. When I go into prison institutions, I just treat the officers and officials the way I'd want to be treated myself—as a valuable human being.

"Instead of assuming any right or privilege, I first go to the classification officer, respecting his or her position of responsibility. From them, I learn their proper procedure of operation. Not all institutions, even in the same region, operate the same way.

"I must also recognize that most classification officers are desperately overloaded, often carrying the cases of 200 men or more at one time. They may also be disillusioned and discouraged, seeing little positive results or appreciation for their labors. They see the system as failing and may feel guilt, frustration, and hopelessness.

"I've had to come to realize that ministry to these officers is just as important as getting my inmate interview. This has freed me to be patient with them and use the waiting time for prayer and expressing love and concern for them."

With this attitude, our counselor is not only helping those who come to The Bridge, but all the men in the prison system. For the prison environment will be largely affected by the attitude of those in authority. No wonder the Apostle Paul wrote from prison, "I exhort therefore, that first of all, supplications, prayers, intercessions, and giving of thanks be made for all men; for kings and for all that are in authority" (I Tim. 2:1,2).

Today, The Bridge has a reputation among Department of Corrections officials as being one the finest and strictest work release programs in the state. They know The Bridge program has more structure and stricter adherence to rules than other work release programs. This is probably one reason why we've been able to effect early work release for one of Florida's most feared criminals, Jack Murphy, who has been converted to Christ and is now serving at The Bridge.

Do we see the prison official as our friend—someone who needs our help and prayers? Yes, Louie, now I do. Thank you.

XIV.
Where Do We Go From Here?

Recently, a heart-rending letter came across my desk. What really tore at me was knowing that this woman's agony is a reality in the hearts of thousands of mothers throughout the country. She wrote:

"What possibly can be done for my son in prison?

He first got in trouble when he was sixteen. He has been in and out of jail and prison ever since. The only thing I see it doing is shortening his life, destroying both his life and mine. He's now thirty-eight and will soon enter another work release program. His trouble has come through alcohol and drugs, and there's been no help for him.

When he was released before, he had such difficulty because he could find no acceptance by people, employers, etc. Society rejected him due to the mistakes he had made. Nobody accepted him as a friend. What hope can a man have who believes he'll never have a friend?

Shouldn't there be centers where perhaps he and other prisoners can be accepted and have conversation with some decent, law-abiding people that will help them make the cross over back to society? My son is interested now in trying (as he calls it, paying back his debt in life) to help young children not to do as he did with drugs, alcohol, and crime. He can talk from experience and children would listen, he feels. But he needs help for himself first.

Can't something be done? This may be my son's last chance."

What a joy it is to offer this mother and others like her some new hope! But the needs are so great. In every state in America, there is significant prison overcrowding. Faced with the growing prison populations and tightening state budgets, department of correction officials are desperately looking to alternative means of incarceration.

Do you realize that it would be less expensive for the average state to build a campus the size and quality of

Harvard and pay all tuition, housing and food of the residents than it would be to send these same people to its state prisons. On an average, it costs a state $14,000-$15,000/year to imprison one man. It costs an additional $50,000 to build one new cell to house that man.

That is very expensive warehousing to keep "troublemakers" out of our hair. Of those "troublemakers", more than half are imprisoned for non-violent crimes. In fact, three-fourths of first offenders are incarcerated for non-violent offenses.

We've already questioned the potential of society getting any lasting value out of its tax dollars for incarceration. At best, the man leaving prison will be no better off than before his imprisonment. Says Norman Carlson, head of the Federal Bureau of Prison, "I've given up hope for rehabilitation in prison because there's nothing we can do to force change on offenders. Change must come from the heart."

How much better to use our tax dollars to bring more healing, wholeness, and discipleship to Christ to offenders. As of January 1, 1985, 146 men have gone through The Bridge program. Only twelve have been re-arrested and returned to prison.

If, at The Bridge, we are effective with keeping just 75% of the men from returning to prison, we will not only further God's kingdom but save mucho tax dollars. Using the national average of recidivism, The Bridge success rate represents a savings of nearly a million dollars yearly in reduced expenses for prison costs for every 100 men through the program. Add in the expense for additional prison housing and the value of the men working jobs and paying taxes themselves, and the savings are even greater.

Comparing The Bridge to other work release centers in the state and country, they will average just one job/help counselor to every 50 to 150 men. As a result, in many work release centers, over half the men eligible for work do not have jobs. At The Bridge, there is a full-time paid counselor for every seven residents. And so we have been able to get every man coming to The Bridge a job within a week of his arrival. This translates into additional thousands of dollars worth of human resources being used and not wasted.

Perhaps putting the value of aftercare centers in these terms borders on carnality. The greatest value, of course, is the redemption and restoration of human souls for God's kingdom. What God has accomplished at The Bridge can and must be multiplied hundreds of times over in every state in our nation.

What can you do to bring effective prisoner aftercare to your community? Depending on who you are, consider the following suggestions:

1. FOR THE PRISONER:

Consider your own possible need for aftercare. Do you have a "bridge", a support system, to help you cross over into community responsibility and acceptance in a local church? If you are like your fellow inmates, almost all your thinking has been concerned with just getting out of the joint and not what you will do after release. The Bible warns us, "Where there is no vision (plan), the people perish" (Proverbs 29:18).

From reading this book, I hope you can see that making it in society after prison doesn't just automatically happen. The odds are against you making it. But with God's help, you can make it! You do have to have a plan and be willing to allow others to help. The first step of asking for help may be the hardest part. It is a humbling experience, and because of past hurts, you may find it very difficult to trust anyone. God promises us that if we will ask and pray (Matt. 7:7), He will bless and reward us.

How do you go about it? First, talk to your counselor or chaplain about any Christian aftercare centers in your state. In Appendix C of this book, we've included a partial list of Christian aftercare centers that accept ex-offenders. These are just the ones that we are familiar with. If there is one in your state or area, write them and find out more about their program to see if it would benefit you. Realize that most of these centers are not yet working under state contract to qualify as a work release center.

Then pray for the Lord's guidance in your life. God has promised to guide you by His Holy Spirit (John 16:13). He will not fail or forsake you (Hebrews 13:5). Pray also for The Bridge and every aftercare center that God will provide every need and give divine favor before correctional officials.

2. FOR THE CHRISTIAN LAYMAN AND/OR PRISON MINISTRY VOLUNTEER:

Support the vision!

When you share with inmates either by letter or in personal visitation, help them realize their need for that "bridge" upon release. In many ways, you can be that support system. However, realistically determine whether you can commit yourself to all that may be required of you, especially if your inmate friend has no marketable job skills and/or past substance abuse problems.

Then share the aftercare vision with other prison ministry friends and chaplains. If there is a Christian aftercare center in your area, support it. If none exists, intercede and pray that God will raise one up.

Finally, be an involved citizen in your community and state. Realize that it is your vote that creates and maintains your state prison system. If it is backward and antiquated, talk to your government officials about what can be done. Find out where they stand on prison reform and vote for those who support positive rehabilitation. When there are public commissions to study where to build new prisons or referendums to allocate huge sums for prison expansion, get involved and suggest alternatives.

For too long, we've thought that we could entrust all governmental problems to the "experts" and they would solve them. Our present prison system is in trouble. Rehabilitation isn't working. God's plan was never rehabilitation; it is regeneration. And God has anointed the church, to minister to prisoners, as Jesus declared, "I was in prison, and ye visited me" (Matt. 25:36).

3. FOR THOSE INTERESTED IN STARTING AN AFTERCARE CENTER:

Pray that God will do this.

If after at least one month of constant prayer and intercession, you are convinced that God wants you involved in starting an aftercare center, I suggest you contact me at Christian Prison Ministries, 2100 Brengle Avenue, Orlando,

Florida 32808.

My staff and I will sit down with you here at The Bridge and pursue your situation. We are committed to continual training of our staff at The Bridge, so our present staff can spin off every one to two years to start other centers. This training includes hands-on experience both at The Bridge and Dunklin Memorial Camp.

Remember, effective aftercare starts with equipped people; then comes a planned program, and finally, building facilities. Don't be tempted to put the cart before the horse by getting a building before the first two are in place.

Not long ago we had a Thanksgiving gathering that included the men at The Bridge. Opportunity was given for each person to share the thing for which they were most thankful. To my surprise and embarrassment, man after man stood to his feet and declared, "I am thankful for Frank Costantino. For without him, there would be no Bridge to come to, and I wouldn't have met Jesus and gotten my life on the right road."

One last man stood and said, "Frank, I'm standing in the middle of your dream. I want to thank you for having the courage to make your dream a reality." This was a man whose life was radically changed, and now whose children would be eternally changed.

Through my tears, I wanted to rise and protest, "But it wasn't me, it was Jesus!" And then the Lord spoke to my heart, "Yes, it was Me. But I did it through a weak but yielded vessel. And that's a greater miracle. So go ahead and let them lift you up. In so doing, I'm being lifted up even more. For what I'm doing in you, I will do in others."

Yes, I see it clearly—more than a miracle—the story of aftercare expanded and in action everywhere.

Appendix B
Plain Talk in Hard Places

I trust that you are reading this last chapter because either you are already involved in aftercare in some way or you are interested in starting an aftercare facility. As we have said previously, the greatest resource needed for effective aftercare is godly people. God never started with a program but always with a man (or woman).

First, just ask yourself, what are you prepared to give God to accomplish this task? It is my conviction that when we seek to start anything in God's kingdom, we never see the whole picture; it is always bigger than we thought; and it always demands more than we are prepared to give. This is especially true in aftercare.

The law of entropy tells us that everything in our universe tends to move toward randomness. Left to itself, nothing falls together, it always falls apart. So you can see that aftercare ministry requires constant prayer and constant attention. Nothing will work out right on its own, no matter how we hope for good luck.

Our natural nature is to always pay the easiest cost but our best cost is usually the greatest one. A large ministry coalition recently did an extensive research project on what were the problems of the ghetto. Their results of three years of investigation: "Partial answers usually bring total failure. The key to solving the ghetto's problems is to bring total answers to a total area all at once."

So it is with aftercare. If you want to bring wholeness, you must be prepared to minister wholeness. It is not just a spiritual task. It is clothing, feeding, working, playing, and on and on. Someone has said, "Walking in the Spirit is when the supernatural becomes natural." Being an aftercare leader requires walking in the Spirit all day every day.

To put it bluntly, before you start effective aftercare, you should consider: "How many 'rebels' am I willing to bear with, pray for, discipline, father and baby until God performs His miracles in their lives?"

In nearly every other church setting, the "flock" is an asset or giving unit to the pastor or leader, but here every man starts the program as a liability. Our task and challenge is to work with them until they become an asset. This may take many months, and during that time, every aftercare director and counselor must be willing, even desirous, to be used and often misused even as Christ was, to implant the seeds of love, success, and productivity in each life.

The mindset of the aftercare leader must be different from the average pastor who concentrates on the "ninety-nine". The aftercare pastor/counselor must lay down his life for his one or two or five or ten sheep.

Our aftercare director, Mark, says, "So often I've been hurt and wanted to give up, and even did once, because the guys would use me without even a thank you and turn around and screw up. I think most all of us start out in this ministry, at least partially, because we want the guys to make it for our own ego boost. That attitude, however, will kill you fast. The bottom line is that it is their lives, not ours, and if they screw up, it is still their lives. We are just here to give and be used of God until the residents can become healthy and be used too, to help others."

What Mark went through on one hand, I went through on the other. When God called me to go back to prison to minister, I argued with Him, "But God, I don't even like convicts. I've had to spend five years with them and live with all their garbage." I thought not having a bleeding heart for cons would be a disadvantage. I'm not so sure now. I see it very dangerous to be enamoured by your own ministry, especially in aftercare. There must be a total release of the results of God.

This attitude is critical. A good program, even a committed attitude toward aftercare, is not enough. Remember, God had the best program and rules (the Ten Commandments) and he certainly was committed, but until God's higher law of sacrificial love through Christ was revealed, there was no change in the hearts of men.

When we look in a man's life and recognize areas of weakness and shortcomings, what right have we to ask, even demand, that he change? Unless that counselor has surrendered his own weaknesses to God and received the power of God's love both for himself and the men, he will not receive the needed respect where he can be the godly vessel of impartation.

When George, one of our best counselors at The Bridge, first came, he had faith to believe God could do anything for any man. God had divinely healed his own body from crippling arthritis, delivered him from a life sentence, and used him to win every person in his cellblock to Christ. George came to The Bridge and said and did the right things but never won the respect of the men until he allowed the love, discipline, grace and mercy of God to work in the needed areas of his own life. Today, George is just as strict as ever with the men, but now they can receive it with respect, because God's anointing on George bears witness to the truth that it is worked in himself.

George learned (as we all must) that everything we receive from God—grace, mercy, forgiveness, salvation— is free, but nothing that we give or communicate is free. Just as it can cost God dearly to give us these things, it will cost us our will, our very selves, to give them to others. We must be willing to let them be worked in and through us— to go through the mill and the winepresses—before they can become wine and bread of life to others.

Now at The Bridge, much of the exhortation and admonishment is done brother to brother, resident to resident. Regularly, the men do sociograms where they grade each other as the most improved, least improved, most open, most closed, the most energetic, and the laziest. The hard workers are applauded and the stragglers are put on the hot seat and admonished to get with the program. This really works, but only because the atmosphere of love and caring has already been established through counselors.

This is not to say that there are no discipline problems at The Bridge. With 26 men, getting cooperative obedience from them all is a constant challenge. The counselors must use all the power of the rules, rewards, privileges, and deterrents to curb rebellion, all the while they are planting new seeds of love and truth.

Through this, there develops tremendously close ties between men in an aftercare center and their leaders— often much stronger than family (partly because most never had a family or have been totally rejected by family).

The Jim Jones tragedy shows us what can happen when the appreciation of leadership is not properly released to God's Spirit.

This is one reason why I urge that deliverance not be done on a novice level, though most men coming into an aftercare center do need inner healing and some deliverance. When a man opens up and shares things that he has never shared with anyone before, the listener becomes accountable that they do not misuse that information or trust. To do so could be so devastating as to destroy that person.

This is why, I believe, the Catholic Church has appointed confessors—mature people who accepted the vow of confidentiality. To break the vow meant being banned from the church. They realized it wasn't good to let just anyone have that kind of power in a person's life.

Just as dangerous as being caught up with one's ministry is to be overburdened with it. If one cannot release people and their failures to God, they will never survive the aftercare. I like to relate Jesus' parable of sowing the seed (in Mark 4) to our aftercare work. Here Jesus said that only 25% of the soil (lives) into which the seed (God's Word) was sown would be received in such a way to bear harvest.

Now certainly in our intake interviewing we try to discern which men have fertile hearts. But you can't always tell, any more than you can tell if there are rocks or not under the topsoil. Additionally, in some, we may be only used to prepare the ground for someone else to harvest or, as with Jimmy Moore, for the man to return later for fruitfulness: "The word of the Lord came unto Jonah a second time" (Jonah 3:1).

Another aspect of not being overburdened by the ministry is to receive the responsibility of it joyfully and with appreciation. Never see it as a burden. When I was in prison, I wrote an article for our newspaper on the privilege of responsibility. It had become clear to me when the judge proclaimed, while sentencing me to prison, "You aren't a responsible human being. We (society) can't trust you to take care of yourself. So we are going to have the state take care of you for about twenty years, so you will learn to appreciate the privilege of being responsible." Actually, for many convicts, it isn't that they don't appreciate responsibility; nobody has ever taken time to teach them. Responsibility (self-control) is one of the fruits of the Holy Spirit. It can be taught.

Your attitude of joyfully accepting your position as leader, as the responsible one, can make that training attractive to the residents. If you see your responsibilities as a drag instead of a gift of God, that is what you'll communicate, and the men won't want that.

I'm sure that none of you will start out with a "burdened" attitude, but it can easily become that way without good planning of your aftercare center. That's why I suggest you start with a manageable-size (5-15) center. The image of aftercare has been severely tarnished already in certain areas of our country where well-intentioned leaders have begun projects on a grandiose scale only to see them crash to pieces because of poor planning, community resistance, or ill-trained staff.

Staff is another reason to start with a small manageable size. As the size of the aftercare center grows, you will need multi-staff leadership. It takes time to mold together even a well-trained staff where they can minister in one Spirit, in one accord.

I'm convinced it's more worthwhile, whenever possible, to take the time to train and disciple your own supportive staff rather than hire professional counselors or sociologists and hope they are called of God and can effectively work into aftercare. It would be nice if you could just go out and hire aftercare professionals, but there aren't any around.

Begin manageably and begin responsibly. We already discussed that most of the men at The Bridge come by state contract while still under sentence from the Department of Corrections. This is undoubtedly the best arrangement and controls with which to work with the men. They know that if they violate the rules, lay out from work, and/or abuse alcohol or drugs, it is back to prison.

So often there needs to be this deterrent. The men we are working with have not learned to rule their own spirits (and flesh). Satan attacks these men with "impulse temptation"—a flirting girl on the street or a tempting offer of alcohol or drugs from an "old friend" and suddenly, all the work you've done is down the drain.

The only way that I've seen aftercare work effectively where men are not under state "obligation" are programs like Dunklin Memorial Camp and Rehrersburg Teen Challenge Farm, where if a man is tempted to rebel or give up, he must walk fifteen miles to the nearest community to leave. The thought of that walk can defuse many of those impulse errors.

Being out in the country makes it more difficult to provide transportation to needed employment, supplies, etc. These obstacles can be overcome with extra effort easier than the impulse temptation problems.

Again, your first cost is your best cost. Therefore, I urge you to take the extra time to build the relationship with your state correctional system to be able to get men under sentence contract. The extra effort you apply on the front end will make your program so much more effective.

These final words of caution have not been meant in any way to deter or discourage you from aftercare ministry. The desire of my heart is for effective aftercare ministries to be established in every state and large community in America. To be effective, they must be called and ordained of God. To the end, I pray for you, and offer myself as servant, together with you, in His great kingdom!

Appendix A
Application for The Bridge

(For more room, this application may be enlarged on copier.)

Personal History

1. Name _____ S.S.# _____
       (first)   (middle)   (last)

2. Institutional Number _____

3. Date of Birth _____ Place of Birth _____

4. Parent's Name (if living) _____

5. Parent's Address _____
            P.O. Box or Street No.   City   State   Zip

Are your parents separated or divorced? _____Yes _____No

reason: _____

7. Do you possess a driver's license? _____Yes _____No

type:_____ state:_____ number:_____

8. Other rehabillitation centers attended (other than prisons)

   A. Where_____ When_____

   B. Where_____ When_____

   C. Where_____ When_____

   D. Where_____ When_____

   E. Where_____ When_____

9. Number of times you have stayed in a mission: _____

10. Do you have any medical problems? _____Yes _____No

List and describe all medical problems:

_____

_____

_____

11. Any physical problems or limitations? _____ Yes _____ No
List and describe physical problems or limitations below:

_____

_____

_____

12. Do you use alcoholic beverages? _____ Yes _____ No

_____ Occasionally   Explain: _____

13. Do you consider yourself an alcoholic? _____ Yes _____ No

14. Have you ever attended an AA meeting? _____ Yes _____ No

15. Do you use any type(s) of drugs? _____ Yes _____ No

_____ Occasionally   Explain: _____

16. If you are a naturalized citizen, please give the following:

   A. certificate _____

   B. date entered the U.S. (month, year) _____

   C. where issued (city, state) _____

   D. date of final papers (month/day/year) _____

17. Do you receive any of the following:

   Social Security Check ☐

   Veterans Check ☐

   Disability Check ☐

Other _____

APPENDIX A

Prison History

1. Present Institution: Name _____

Address _____

City_____ State_____ Zip _____

2. Your institutional number: _____

3. Check one of the following: Will you be on...

Probation ☐ Parole ☐ Contract Parole ☐ Work Release ☐

4. Proposed release or parole date _____

5. How long will you be on parole, probation, contract parole or work release? _____

6. How many times have you been incarcerated (list below):

Institution	City	State	Date

7. Give three references in the institution (not inmates):

Name	Position

8. List all charges, convictions, and other depositions received, giving dates, places, outcome:

Offense	Place	Date	Sentence

_____

_____

_____

_____

_____

_____

_____

_____

Employment History

*Date Available for work: _____

1. What job training did you have before incarceration?

Job Corps ☐   Manpower ☐   Vocational Training ☐

Other _____

2. Explain each training and where: _____

_____

_____

3. What was your last legal job before incarceration?

Job Title _____ Employer _____

City _____ State _____

Duties performed: _____

APPENDIX A

4. What Jobs have you worked on in the institution?

Institution	Job	How long?

5. What vocational training program did you participate in?

How long? _____

Did you receive a certificate? _____

6. List all courses taken while incarcerated (if shorthand or typing, give speed at course completion)

7. Prior to incarceration, how many hours per day did you work?

8. List your preferences of employment:

1st preference _____

2nd preference _____

3rd preference _____

9. List all skills you have below:

10. List all machines, equipment, tools you have experience with:

_____

_____

_____

11. If you get a job where tools are needed, do you have any?

_____Yes _____No _____able to purchase

12. Have you ever been fired for drinking or quit because of alcohol? Explain: _____

_____

13. Have you ever received Workman's Compensation?

_____Yes _____No

14. Have you ever taken a Civil Service examination?

_____Yes _____No

Family History

1. Marital Status: _____married _____single

   _____separated _____divorced _____widower

2. Wife's name_____ Date of Birth_____

Address_____ Phone_____

3. How long separated? _____

   How long divorced? _____

4. Has your ex-wife remarried? _____Yes _____No

5. What was the reason for your divorce? _____

_____

APPENDIX A

6. How long have you been married? _____

7. Number of times you have been married _____
   If more than once complete the information below:

When Married   When Divorced

(1) _____

(2) _____

(3) _____

Reasons for divorce:

(1) _____

(2) _____

(3) _____

8. Number of children (state which marriage) _____

Names _____

Ages _____

Sex _____

9. Where are your children now? _____

_____

10. If a widower, what was the date of your wife's death? _____

Cause of death? _____

11. List all dependents you have to support, including yourself:

Name   Relationship   Age

_____

_____

_____

_____

Military History

1. Which branch of service have you been with? _____

2. Were you drafted? _____ Yes _____ No

   Did you enlist? _____ Yes _____ No

3. What length of time were you in the Armed Forces? _____

4. Which of the following are you? _____ World War II Veteran

   _____ Vietnam Veteran _____ Other

5. Type of discharge: _____

6. Reserve status: _____ Active _____ Inactive _____ Original _____ None

7. Do you have a service-connected disability income?

   _____ Yes _____ No

8. Were you ever court-martialed? _____ Yes _____ No. If yes, please tell why, when and the result of your court-martial:

   _____

   _____

Education History

1. What was the last grade you completed? _____ grade school

   _____ jr. high _____ high school _____ G.E.D. _____ college

   List year and date of graduation: _____

   _____

2. If you completed college, list your degree _____
                                    (type/year)

   major/minor _____ post-graduate _____

   _____

APPENDIX A

3. Did you ever attend any trade schools? ____Yes ____No

What type? _____

Did you graduate? _____

What years did you attend? _____

4. List all colleges or trade schools attended: _____

_____

5. What specialized training did you receive? _____

_____

Medical History

1. What is the state of your physical health? ____excellent

____good ____fair ____poor ____declining

2. What is your height_____, weight_____, usual weight_____?

3. List all major illnesses or operations you have ever had:

_____

_____

_____

4. Are you handicapped in any way? ____Yes ____No. If yes, what type of handicap do you have? _____

5. Do you presently have, or have you ever had, emphysema?

_____Yes _____No

6. Have you ever been hospitalized for alcoholism or drug addiction? _____Yes _____No (Also list related illnesses.)

Where   When

_____

_____

_____

7. Have you ever used drugs other than for medical purposes?

What   How long   Where

_____

_____

_____

8. Are you now taking any medication? _____Yes _____No

What_____How long_____

9. Have you ever been committed to a psychiatric hospital?

_____Yes _____No _____committed _____voluntary admittance

Where were you admitted?_____Date_____

10. Have you ever had a severe emotional upset?____Yes____No

What was the cause? _____

11. Do you have hospital insurance? ____Yes ____No

With whom? _____

What is your medicare # _____

What is your medicaid # _____

APPENDIX A

Religious History

1. Are you a church member? _____

2. Have you ever been a church member? _____

3. What denomination? _____ Where _____

4. What is your pastor's name? _____

5. How often did you attend? _____

6. Are you a Christian? ____yes ____no ____not sure

7. How often do you read the Bible? _____

8. Have you ever been baptized? _____

9. When did you become a Christian? _____

10. What is your chaplain's name? _____

11. Do you pray? _____ When? _____

12. Please give the religious background of your family when you were growing up:

_____

_____

_____

I hereby attest that I have answered all questions honestly and to the best of my ability.

_____ _____
            Name   Date

Ministry Agreement
between

_____

and
THE BRIDGE

Christian Prison Ministries, Inc. is presently operating a comprehensive discipleship program, herein after called The Bridge.

The Bridge has the staff and facilities to provide a high quality of rehabilitative services to individuals in need of such services.

The Bridge will provide for the following services:
1. Appropriate living quarters
2. Regular counseling
3. Assistance in job placement
4. Assistance in transportation in getting to and from work.
5. Food service will be provided at the expense of the resident unless the resident is not employed. In that case, food will be provided free of charge.
6. Regular group meetings for the purpose of rehabilitation.

Services Desired By The Resident

We at The Bridge have divided the areas of our ministry to the resident into four categories. These categories are as follows: spiritual, mental, physical, and social. In the following section of this agreement is listed areas in each category which the resident sees the need to work on and gives permission to the staff at The Bridge to minister into these problem areas.

Services offered by The Bridge in order to achieve Resident's Goals

I. Spiritual

II. Mental

III. Physical

IV. Social

Along with these services, the resident will be required to keep all the rules of The Bridge and attend all meetings, unless otherwise stated by the director of the center.

APPENDIX A

I, _____, make a commitment to God, and myself, and the staff at The Bridge, to earnestly pursue the goals I have set forth for myself while I remain at The Bridge. I am willing to commit myself to a period of _____ months as a resident of The Bridge.

This agreement may be revised with the joint permission of the resident, and his counselor, and the director of the center.

The staff may cancel this agreement at anytime when they feel the resident is not trying to improve himself and is not cooperating with the spirit of the program at The Bridge.

I, _____ on the _____ day of the month of _____, enter into this agreement with God, the staff, and other residents of The Bridge discipleship center of Christian Prison Ministries, Inc.

_____
resident

_____
director

_____
counselor

APPENDIX A

Agreement to abide by the rules of
The Bridge

I, _____, have read over the rules of The Bridge discipleship center, and I have had them explained to me by a staff person of The Bridge discipleship center.

I agree to abide by all the rules of The Bridge discipleship center for as long as I am a resident there.

_____
resident

_____
director

_____
counselor

_____
date

Appendix C
Aftercare Center Directory

ALASKA
Teen Challenge/Alaska
236 West 10th St.
Anchorage, AK 99501
Duane Guisinger
(907) 277-2914

Applicant must express sincere desire to establish solid relationship with Jesus Christ

ALABAMA
Outreach Ministries of AL
P.O. Box 3194
Huntsville, AL 35810

Please write for brochure

ARKANSAS
Teen Challenge of Arkansas
P.O. Box 8177
Hot Springs, AR 71909

Staff must interview applicants before acceptance

The Way Home
Route 5, Box 5165
Venton, AR 72015
Don Mott

ARIZONA
Teen Challenge
P.O. Box 593
Cave Creek, AZ 85331

Will not consider ex-offenders with violent crime involvement

Teen Challenge of Arizona
4444 E. Grant Rd., #106
P.O. Box 5966
Tucson, AZ 85703

Springboard Shelter Care
3644 N. Nufer Place
Tucson, AZ 85705
Janet Stone

Short term, 1 week to 1 month, ages 7-18 w/court approval

Teen Challenge of Tucson
729 N. 4th Ave.
Tucson, AZ 85705

Drug & alcohol related problems

CALIFORNIA

Centrum of Hollywood
P.O. Box 29069
Hollywood, CA 90029
Joseph Appler, Dir.
(213) 463-5576

Temporary Housing,
Crisis Intervention,
Referral Ministry

Fellowship Vine Ministry
845 N. Holliston Ave.
Pasadena, CA 91104
Nick Cadena

No court cases pending.
No sexual offenders. Must write
for application packet and rules
& regulations

Victory Outreach
P.O. Box 1248, 10548 Tuxford St.
Sun Valley, CA 91352
Jon Saenz

Christian rehabilitation

House of Magdalene
P.O. Box 3005
N. Hollywood, CA 91609

Female ex-offenders,
interview with candidate for
acceptability required.

Teen Challenge
1304 24th St., P.O. Box 8087
San Diego, CA 92102

Inmate contact required
6 months prior to release

Ventura Teen Challenge
P.O. Box 1064
Ventura, CA 93002
Herb Davis

Females, ages 18-50, drug
and/or alcohol related. Contact
by mail.

Kern County Teen Challenge
326 South H St.
Bakersfield, CA 93304

Commitment to one year
Christian Rehab. Program

New Life for Girls
329 N. Yosemite
Fresno, CA 93701
Cheryl Sadelson

Sincere desire to change
old way of life

Teen Challenge
1464 Valencia
San Francisco, CA 94110
Dick Rhoads, Dir.
285-1353

Live-in, 9-month to one-year
program

APPENDIX C

Love in Action
P.O. Box 2655
San Rafael, CA 94903

Application & reference
procedure a must. State work
background & church attendance
Some pre-counseling by our staff

Teen Challenge
P.O. Box 28464
San Jose, CA 95159
Gwen Wilkerson
(408) 275-8240

Women, ages 18 up

Lighthouse Ranch
Rt. 1, Box 28
Loleta, CA 95551
Jay Crowdus
(707) 733-5558

Personal and/or telephone
interviews with candidate,
candidate's pastor, and parole
officer.

CANADA
Turning Point Girls' Home
High Road RR 1, Ridgeway
Ontario, CD LOS-INO
Larry Snider
(416) 894-0671

Ages 16-20, not pregnant,
life controlling problems

Hamilton Teen Challenge
P.O. Box 536, Hamilton
Ontario, CD L8N 3H8
George T. Glover, Dir.
(416) 526-1414

Must submit to rules &
regulations of Teen
Challenge program

Covenant House/Under 21
70 Gerrard St. E, Toronto
Ontario, CD M5B 1G6

Ages under 21, no alcohol or
drugs, open intake policy

COLORADO
Teen Challenge
1746 Emerson
Denver, CO 80218

Must make 1 year commitment,
and complete info. packet
provided for screening process

Teen Challenge
P.O. Box 5000
Woodland Park, CO 80866

Must submit application
for approval

CONNECTICUT
Youth Challenge
15-17 May St.
Hartford, CT 06105

Interview required, desires to change life, submission to rules & regulations

Exodus Ministries, Inc.
P.O. Box 616
Winstead, CT 06098

Girls must be willing to submit to our schedule and make a serious commitment to a new beginning

Pivot Re-entry Program
17 Quintard Ave.
South Norwalk, CT 06854

Males, 16 years or older Approved for admission by personal interview

FLORIDA
N. Florida Teen Challenge
1409 Cherry St.
Jacksonville, FL 32205

Males, ages 18-34
Do not work with homosexuals

Our Father's House
1012 N. Palafox
Pensacola, FL 32501
(903) 434-7860

Women, women with children, & couples

The Bridge
2100 Brengle
Orlando, FL 32808
Frank Costantino

Prisoner Aftercare

Turning Point Ministry
13650 Walsingham Road
Largo, FL 33544
Rev. Jack Hosman
(813) 596-7600

A Christian drug rehabilitation program for adolescents. Write for brochure.

Teen Challenge of Florida
Rt. 1, Box 1460
Avon Park, FL 33825

One year program. Girls only, ages 18-35. Must provide own transportation should person decide to leave.

GEORGIA
Swede's Prison Ministry
P.O. Box 456
Kennesaw, GA 30144
Chaplain Swede Swanson

APPENDIX C

New Life Center
P.O. Box 42346
Atlanta, GA 30311

Applicants must be serious about changing their lives. Must be interviewed before acceptance.

Paul Anderson Youth Home
P.O. Box 525
Vidalia, GA 30474
Paul Anderson

Young men, ages 15-18

HAWAII

Teen Challenge Maui
P.O. Box 250
Wailuka, HI 96793

Write for brochure and admissions policy

Teen Challenge Oahu
P.O. Box 434
Honolulu, HI 96809
Chas. E. McDonald

Applicants must be interviewed before consideration

Youth With A Mission
Box 122
Honolulu, HI 96826

IOWA

Teen Challenge
3650 Cottage Grove
Des Moines, IA 50311

Ages 18-30, male only, 14 month program

Iowa Safe House
Rt. 1
Humboldt, IA 50548
Phil Schenck
(515) 332-2050

Women, ages 18-30 with a sincere desire to change their lives. Referral for men available.

ILLINOIS

Elder Jerry Hodges
9418 S. Racine Ave.
Chicago, IL 60620
Jerry Hodges
(312) 779-2284

Life for Girls
2437 N. Lowell
Chicago, IL 60639

Voluntary program, 13 months.
Must abide by house rules.
Phone interview required before
acceptance.

Jesus People-USA-FGM
4707 N. Malden
Chicago, IL 60640

Interview with staff member
required before acceptance.

INDIANA
Jesus Inside Prison Ministry
109 W. 21st St.
Indianapolis, IN 46202
William Bumphus
(317) 925-6884

Daystar Ministries
P.O. Box 1514
Martinsville, IN 46151
Doug Easterday

Write for rules & regulations,
admissions information, cost

Indianapolis Teen Challenge
2542 N. Delaware
Indianapolis, IN 47302

Women only, must have received
Christ in prison & show
long-term fruits.

KANSAS
Light House for Girls
RR 1
Gem, KS 27734
(913) 422-7849

LOUISIANA
Louisiana Teen Challenge
1905 Franklin Ave.
New Orleans, LA 70117

Monitored housing, 4-month
program. Assists with housing
& job placement

Fellowship Mission Center
P.O. Box 3311
Shreveport, LA 71133-3311
Rev. Bobby Henderson
(318) 226-9393

Prisoner rehabilitation;
prisoner aftercare; work release
center

MASSACHUSETTS

New England Teen Challenge
P.O. Box 3265, 1315 Main St.
Brockton, MA 02403

Applicant must be willing to submit to rules & program structures. Male & Female.

MARYLAND

Teen Challenge
6900 Central Ave.
Capitol Heights, MD 20743

Write for brochure

Someone Who Cares
11604 Georgia Ave.
Wheaton, MD 20902
Rev. Dr. Jacoba S. Quinn
(301) 942-5262

MICHIGAN

Ionia Bible Church
706 W. Main St.
Ionia, MI 48846
Rick Martin
(616) 527-6827

MINNESOTA

New Hope Center
212 11th Ave. S.
Minneapolis, MN 55415
(612) 333-1589

2 month Christian live-in program, drug or alcohol related problems.

Midwest Challenge
8200 Grand Ave. S.
Minneapolis, MN 55420

16-30 year old males

Damascus Way, Inc.
3361 Republic Ave.
St. Louis Park, MN 55426

Men, 18 years & older. Write for more information.

MISSOURI

Faith, Hope & Love Ministry
8967 Old Lemoy Ferry Rd.
Hillsboro, MO 63050
Alvin Hanson

Very limited live-in. Must be evaluated before acceptance.

Mid-America Teen Challenge
P.O. Box 1089
Cape Girardeau, MO 63701

Must complete program once enrolled.

Teen Challenge
P.O. Box 429 J.S.
Springfield, MO 65801
(417) 864-6305

Write for acceptance requirements.

NORTH CAROLINA
Grtr. Pdmt. Teen Challenge
P.O. Box 7795
Greensboro, NC 27407

Drug or alcohol abuse. Applicant must be willing to "get it together" and make a commitment of 1½ years to complete the program.

Gethsemane Rainbow
P.O. Box 19647
Raleigh, NC 27619
Patricia McCallum
(919) 821-5433

Eight residents maximum, 90 day terms, donations requested

NEBRASKA
Teen Challenge
2916 N. 58th St.
Omaha, NE 68104

Must be aware of rules & submit to them and authority. Women's Center

NEW HAMPSHIRE
His Mansion
P.O. Box 40
Hillsboro, NH 03244

Write for brochure

NEW JERSEY
Bethel Home for Girls
29 New Street
Nutley, NJ 07110

Write for information & policies

Mission Teens, Inc.
P.O. Box 131
Glendora, NJ 08029

Must be willing to seek God as the answer to their problems

NEW MEXICO
Victory Outreach
145 Madison NE
Albuquerque, NM 87101

Reach Out To Jesus
521 8th Street
Albuquerque, NM 87102
Curtis Ware

New Life, Inc.   Drug & alcohol related
P.O. Box 25387   rehabilitation. Write for
Albuquerque, NM 87215   brochure
Michael Campbell

NEW YORK
Under 21-New York   Short term program
460 W. 41st Street
New York, NY 10036

Hope Christian Center   Induction center for Teen
P.O. Box 189, 1444 Bryant Ave.   Challenge. Applicant must
Bronx, NY 10459   be willing to go through
                                  entire 14 month program

Walter Hoving Home   17 & older, drug, alcohol &
P.O. Box 194   court-related cases. Girls only.
Garrison, NY 10524

Crossroads Ministry, Inc.   Agreement to abide by rules &
802 Kent Ave.   regulations and be open to
Brooklyn, NY 11205   Gospel of Jesus Christ
Rev. Richard Calarie

Teen Challenge   Ex-offenders from county
Box 72 Colvin Sta.   facilities only (no state)
124 Furman
Syracuse, NY 13205
David Pilch

Buffalo Teen Challenge   Applicants must be able to read
500 Leroy Ave.   & write and be willing to change
Buffalo, NY 14215
Don Swartzlander

Rochester Teen Challenge   Must submit application, and
75 Alexander St.   have either personal or phone
Rochester, NY 14620   interview

OHIO

Teen Challenge for Girls
P.O. Box 2
Columbus, OH 43216

18 years of age or older; drug, alcohol, or repeat offender related; voluntary program; not pregnant

Lamb Ministries
130 Cleveland Street
Youngstown, OH 44515
Rev. Fred Mayhew
(216) 746-2911

Rehabilitation from a Christian approach; applicant must be willing to make a serious commitment to program.

Cincinnati Teen Challenge
P.O. Box 249
Milford, OH 45150
Marylin Baughman

Rehabilitation for hard-core drug addicts, male, ages 18-30

OKLAHOMA

Christ Bars None Ranch
Rt. 1 Box 434-C
Noble, OK 73068

Age limit to 18. Boys ranch.

PENNSYLVANIA

Teen Challenge Harrisburg
1421 N. Front Street
Harrisburg, PA 17102

Inmates must write every 2 weeks for a 2-month period prior to release. People on street can arrange 24-hour interview.

New Life for Girls, Inc.
P.O. Box d-700
Dover, PA 17315
Molly Smith

Women only; desire to turn their lives around; voluntary unless sentenced by judge

Teen Challenge
239 E. Wister
Philadelphia, PA 19144
(215) 843-2887

Life controlling problems; drug, alcohol, immorality & crime related

Teen Challenge Training Ctr.
P.O. Box 98
Rehrersburg, PA 19550
(717) 933-4181

Must complete local induction center program before admission.

SOUTH CAROLINA

PTL Opportunity Farm
Heritage USA, Bus. Hwy. 21
Fort Mill, SC 29715
Jeffrey Park
(803) 548-2797

8-week aftercare program for ex-offenders.

TENNESSEE

Teen Challenge
P.O. Box 3396
Chattanooga, TN 37404
Dexter Clem
(615) 698-1332

Willing to wait for entry under some form of agreed-on supervision; willing to abide by all rules & regulations

Teen Challenge-Nashville
P.O. Box 23281
Nashville, TN 37702

Drug/alcohol related problems, 14-16 month commitment.

Teen Challenge of Memphis
2114 Union Ave.
Memphis, TN 38105

Will consider ex-offender on same basis as any other candidate

TEXAS

Gates of Life
P.O. Box 862
Van, TX 75790
(214) 569-2443

Ft. Worth Teen Challenge
747 Samuels Ave.
Ft. Worth TX 76102

Females, 12 & older. Must be ready to make commitment to Christ; 8 months to 1 year

Salvation Army Trans. House
2407 N. Main St.
Houston, TX 77009
Israel Jones
(713) 224-4748

Parole and/or mandatory supervision with halfway house mandates

The Shoulder, Inc.
5009 Calhoun Rd.
P.O. Box 4300
Houston, TX 77210-9990

Please write for brochure containing admissions policies, accomodations, qualifications

Teen Challenge Dept. T
P.O. Box 134
Hungerford, TX 77448
Karen Apple
(409) 532-5613

Teen Challenge/S. Texas
Box 671
Wharton, TX 77488
(713) 342-9505

Teen Challenge of S.A.   Must be voluntary; between
Westwood Farm, Rt. 3 Box 61   14 & 17; desperate to change.
Floresville, TX 78114
(512) 393-6762

Teen Challenge of Amarillo   Live-in rehabilitation; life
P.O. Box 508   controlling problems; 18-35.
Amarillo, TX 79105

Teen Challenge   One year 24-hour supervision
P.O. Box 251   program to minister to those
Midland, TX 79702   with life-controlling problems
(915) 682-3244

WASHINGTON
Youth Outreach   Juveniles only, by referral
905 Winchell Ave.   of Juvenile Rehab. or DSHS
Vancouver, WA 98661

WISCONSIN
Life Challenge   Inmate approval required
c/o Solid Rock Ministry
Box 2474
Appleton, WI 54913

WEST VIRGINIA
Teen Challenge for New Life   Ages 13-17, juvenile program,
P.O. Box 2278   approval for admission required
Wheeling WV 26003
Walter Long